D1351755

TAKE THAT
Back for Good

By James McCarthy

ABSTRACT SOUNDS BOOKS LTD

Abstract Sounds Books Ltd
Unit 207, Buspace Studios, Conlan Street, London W10 5AP
www.abstractsoundsbooks.com

Published by Abstract Sounds Books Ltd
Licensed from Archive Media Publishing Ltd
ISBN: 978-0-9566959-1-8

DVD CREDITS

All film interviews are copyright Archive Media Publishing Ltd

BOOK CREDITS

Written by: James McCarthy © Archive Media Publishing Ltd

Book Photography Credits

Wenn: Pages 34, 39, 40, 45, 48, 54, 56, 57, 58, 60, 61, 62, 64, 71, 78, 83, 86, 97, 100, 104, 109, 112, 116

Pictorial Press: Pages 4, 9, 13, 16, 22, 27, 30, 53, 74

Empics: Pages 57, 92

Contents

4 | **TAKE THAT** back for good

Introduction

They are arguably the biggest band of the 90s and of the new millennium, with millions of record sales worldwide and perhaps could be regarded as the greatest pop band of the modern era. They have consisted of five members, then four members and then five members again. They have received awards across the world, had 11 UK number ones and 22 songs which have made the top 40 in the UK alone. They are the one and only Take That.

Take That were formed as a five piece pop band in the late 80s but it wasn't until the early 90s that the band became famous. They originate from all over the country and were formed as part of a nationwide talent search which culminated in auditions in Manchester. The group originally consisted of five members, Robbie Williams, Gary Barlow, Howard Donald, Mark Owen and Jason Orange, although Williams would famously leave the band only to return in 2010. The band has not only had success as a group but also huge successes as solo artists particularly in the case of Williams and Barlow.

Throughout the 90s the band produced hit after hit until in 1996 the band broke up citing personal differences and the desire to pursue solo careers. Williams himself had left a year earlier in 1995 and had already began to forge a highly successful solo career, something which Gary Barlow arguably resented as he felt he was as talented as Williams and arguably the better song writer. The band all had varying degrees of success as solo artists but after a quiet period in the early 2000s, Barlow, Orange, Donald and Owen decided that they would reform in 2005 to do a Take That Greatest Hits Tour. The demand for tickets was enormous and led to the band deciding to properly reform in 2006.

Between 2006 and 2010 the band had numerous chart successes and became a household name to a whole new generation of teenagers. The bedroom walls that had been plastered with posters of the young twenty somethings for the 90s generation were now becoming filled with posters again for the noughties generation as well. Williams himself was having troubles with both his musical career and personal life and had turned to drink. After a period of rehabilitation, rumours started to surface in 2008 that Barlow and Williams had patched up their differences and that the two were planning for Robbie to return. The rumours died down until 2010 when tabloids said the two were planning to release a new song and that Robbie would re-join Take That for an album in 2010 and a tour.

Their dance-oriented pop tunes and soulful ballads dominated the UK charts in the first half of the 1990s, spawning two of the best-selling albums of the decade with Everything Changes which was nominated for the 1994 Mercury Prize and Greatest Hits 1996, and according to All Music, "at this time were giant superstars in Europe with the main question about them not being about whether they could get a hit single, but how many and which would make it to number one". The band also won multiple BRIT Awards throughout their careers.

However, after a 2005 documentary and the

release of a new greatest hits album, they officially announced a 2006 reunion tour around the United Kingdom, entitled The Ultimate Tour. On 9 May 2006, it was announced that Take That were set to record together as a band once again. Their fourth studio album, Beautiful World was released in 2006 and was followed up with The Circus, released in 2008. Their sixth studio album, Progress is set for release on 22 November 2010. This will be the first album featuring the original line-up since their 1995 album, Nobody Else.

The group have now regained their place at the top of popular music and are regarded as one of the most significant bands of the past 20 years both musically and lyrically. As we approach a brand new decade, it can be argued that Take That could be hugely significant for three decades of popular music and could shape the future of the genre as a whole. In this book and the accompanying DVDs we will look at where it all went right and wrong for Take That, the awards, sales, successes and failures of the group. We will explore the characters that make up the band and chart the history of five individuals' rise to stardom.

How did Take That define 90s Pop Music?

The 1990s were a hugely significant decade in the development of pop music as a genre and a decade in which pop music regained its likeability with the public. After the teeny boppers and soft melodies that had dominated the 80s, music producers and the public craved for a new movement in pop music, one which combined image, lyrics and perhaps a crossover between rock and roll and pop. In the United Kingdom, this diverse decade saw the continuation of teen pop of the 1980s and the emergence of grunge music and alternative rock in pop culture replacing glam metal and the continuation of hip hop. It also featured the rise of contemporary country music as a major genre, which started in the 1980s.

Whereas the 80s were the era of teen pop, the 90s would become known as the era of the boy band. Music producers such as Nigel Martin-Smith, who created Take That, and Louis Walsh, who created East 17 and later Boyzone and Westlife, had realised that there was a gap in the music market for a crossover group that combined the best of lyrical talent and modern image. Both groups would become the defining features of early 90s pop music and sold records in their millions worldwide. The latter stages of the decade saw the rise in girl bands, a spinoff from the hugely successful boy bands that had dominated. Notably the decade saw the rise of the Spice Girls in 1996, just as both Take That and East 17 were beginning to wind down their music careers and starting to think about become solo artists.

In a poll taken at the end of the decade by Smash Hits Magazine, the top three groups of the 90s were named as The Spice Girls, Take That and East 17, highlighting the sheer dominance that the group had over 90s popular music. Take That defined the genre of 90s pop because they impacted so much on the lives of people who listened to their music. Girls had hundreds of posters all over their walls, there were mad crowds whenever the band made a public appearance and the groups became national icons with hundreds of television appearances both in the UK and abroad. For a band to have such dominance of a genre they have to be considered as one of the all-time great bands in popular music.

Pictorial Press

The band members and their careers in Take That and as soloists

GARY BARLOW

Gary Barlow was born in January of 1971 and is widely regarded as the band's chief songwriter. He was also the producer for most of the band's later work particularly since their reformation in 2006. Barlow is one of Britain's most successful songwriters. He has had two Number 1 hits and a Number 1 album along with five other top 40 UK singles as a solo singer in the last half of the 1990s. In addition to his solo successes Barlow has had eleven Number 1 singles and seven Number 1 albums with Take That. He is a five-time recipient of the prestigious Ivor Novello Award and has been voted the greatest British songwriter of all time.

Barlow was born in Frodsham, a small town in Cheshire to Marjorie and Colin Barlow, Gary also had an older brother called Ian. Barlow's passion for music is said to come from his childhood when he used to watch music on television all the time and would never miss on episode of Top of The Pops. In addition he used to listen constantly to pop music on the radio and said that one of his inspirations to start a career in music was the Depeche Mode song "Just Can't Get Enough".

He married his long term girlfriend Dawn Andrews in January of 2000; she had originally worked as a backing dancer during Take That's

1995 "Nobody Else" Tour. They have three children: Daniel, Emily and Daisy. Barlow is a popular believer in the law of attraction and credits this theory of thought with much of his success. He revealed in his autobiography that he is a supporter of Liverpool FC with their anthem You'll Never Walk Alone being one of the first songs he learned to play on piano.

In his autobiography My Take, Barlow mentions he was on the Edgware Road tube train that was one of the targets of the 7 July 2005 London bombings. In 2009, Barlow named "Don't Give Up", the 1986 duet between Peter Gabriel and Kate Bush, as the song that had most inspired him. He said: "I don't think you can listen to this song without feeling inspired, it could save anybody. The lyrics are so inspirational. Specifically I was having a very low moment in the 1990s and the song came on the radio. There have only been a very few times when I've had to pull the car over to listen to a song – this was one of them."

Barlow got a keyboard for Christmas at the age of ten and started to teach himself how to read music and play both the keyboard and later the piano. In 1986 Barlow entered a BBC Pebble Mill at One competition called A Song For Christmas with a song called Let's Pray For Christmas. After getting through to the semi-finals, he was invited to London's West Heath Studios to record his song.

He then embarked on the traditional route for an aspiring musician by entering the club scene in his local town and area. Gary Barlow's first performance was at the Connah's Quay Labour Cub in the late eighties. In 1989 he appointed Wigan show business agent Barry Woolley to be his manager and recorded a single titled "Love Is In The Air" under the stage name Kurtis Rush. After the single's commercial failure, Barlow was dropped by Woolley. After a period of playing low key venues in the North of England, Barlow came under the influence of pop manager Nigel Martin-Smith and formed Take That, becoming the lead singer. He was introduced to Martin-Smith by Manchester photographer Michael Braham whom Barlow paid to take publicity shots. Braham, an aspiring actor at the time, was also represented by Martin-Smith and knew he was looking for members to form a pop group.

After joining Take That, Barlow became renowned as one of the finest songwriters of his generation and penned numerous number one hits for the group. His first written number one was the single "Pray" which followed on from top ten hits with "Could it be Magic" and "It only takes a Minute". Barlow had become a superstar and some people were beginning to call him the next George Michael.

After the band disbanded in 1996, Barlow was

predicted to do the best out of a future solo career. His first two solo singles Forever Love and Love Won't Wait both leapt to the number one spot in his home country. Forever Love was also used as the soundtrack to the film The Leading Man. His debut album Open Road reached number 1 in the UK Album Chart. Barlow's first ever single to be released in the United States as a solo artist was So Help Me Girl which reached Number 44 on the Billboard Hot 100 Singles Chart. He then achieved another top ten hit in the UK with Open Road peaking at number 7.

After the success of his first solo album he released his second LP Twelve Months, Eleven Days in 1999. Barlow released Stronger as the lead single preceding the album however due to an expected backlash against Barlow, because of his negative comments towards Robbie Williams, it received minimal promotion and airplay and peaked at number 16. The second single For All That You Want again was subjected to minimal radio play and peaked at number 24. Twelve Months, Eleven Days was released soon after the second single to little promotion and peaked at a disappointing number 34, which led to Sony recalling Barlow's 'greatest' song according to critics, the scheduled third single from his second album Lie To Me. This resulted in Barlow and BMG parting company.

Barlow has also been heavily involved in charity work throughout his career being involved in the 2010 Helping Haiti relief song and many appeals for both Children in Need and Comic Relief. Gary organised a sponsored climb to the top of Mount Kilimanjaro to raise money for Comic Relief. Barlow and eight other celebrities: Cheryl Cole, Ben Shepherd, Alesha Dixon, Kimberley Walsh, Fearne Cotton, Chris Moyles, Denise Van Outen and Ronan Keating, made it to the top of Mount Kilimanjaro safely on Sunday 7 March 2009, raising millions for Comic Relief.

Gary's charity efforts in 2009, including his organising of the BT Comic Relief Kilimanjaro Climb and his organising of 'Children In Need Rocks', raised in excess of 6 million pounds. In addition to the charity events organised by Gary, the pop star has also shown support for fellow artists' charity efforts including that of Ronan Keating. The pair belted out Take That's Back For Good at Ronan's Emerald and Ivy Ball in Battersea, South London. The starry bash raised £650,000 for Cancer Research UK. Towards the end of 2009, there was a huge twitter campaign to 'Get Gary Knighted' for all of his charity work over the years. The campaign was mentioned and endorsed by many celebrities, including Chris Moyles of Radio 1.

At the beginning of May 2010, it was announced that Her Majesty Queen Elizabeth II had asked

Pictorial Press

back for good **TAKE THAT** | **13**

Gary Barlow to organise her 85th birthday and her Diamond Jubilee celebrations in 2012. A source said: "Her Majesty has been made well aware of his charity work and the events he has put together. She knows that Gary has got the power to pull in the big names across the music industry and to ensure it's a party to match the occasion".

Barlow combined with Robbie Williams in 2010 for a one off collaboration marking their reunion as friends. The song was called Shame and peaked at number 2 in the UK singles chart.

ROBBIE WILLIAMS

Robbie Williams was born to Peter and Janet Williams in Stoke-on-Trent in February 1974. He and his older sister, Sally, were raised by his mother, Janet, as she and his father, stand-up comedian Peter "Parp" Conway, separated when Williams was three days old and have since divorced. Williams attended Mill Hill Primary School at Stoke-on-Trent then St Margaret Ward Roman Catholic School in Tunstall. Williams realised he had dramatic and musical talents from an early age and also attended dance school UKDDF in Tunstall.

He participated in several school plays, and his biggest role was that of the Artful Dodger in a production of Oliver! A talented footballer, Williams briefly played for Port Vale Football Club before suffering an ankle injury that finished what was a promising career. Following this, and prior to becoming involved in Take That, Williams worked as a double glazing salesman, but he was fired after being caught advising customers not to buy from the company. In 2004 Williams was inducted into the UK music hall of fame and was voted in two separate polls as the greatest artist of the 1990s.

Williams has reportedly battled mental illness, obesity, self-esteem issues, alcoholism, and substance abuse throughout his life. He once discussed how his friend Elton John booked him into a clinic to cope with his drug use that emerged from the depression he was experiencing while still in Take That. He entered a rehabilitation centre in Tucson Arizona for his addiction to prescription drugs and the energy drink Lucozade in 2007. Williams used to smoke up to 60 cigarettes a day, but gave up in 2009 for his girlfriend Ayda Field.

Robbie has undoubtedly had the most success out of any of the band as a solo artist. When he left Take That in 1995, he believed that he would do better without the group and up until about 2003 this appeared to be the case, with Robbie selling millions of records worldwide. He launched his solo career in 1996 with a version of George Michael's "Freedom" which reached number 2 in the UK singles chart. His debut album, Life Thru a Lens, was released in September 1997. The album launched with his first live solo gig at the Élysée Montmartre theatre in Paris, France. At first, the album was slow to take off, debuting at number eleven in the UK Album Charts. The third single of the album, "South of the Border", failed to make a significant impact on the UK Charts. When it was released in September 1997, it reached number fourteen.

After Williams met the record company's concerns about his future, he released what would be the fourth single taken from his album, not knowing it would become his biggest single in the United Kingdom so far, and one of his most well-known songs and successful. "Angels" became Williams's best-seller in the United Kingdom, being certified double platinum. The song, apart from becoming a hit around Europe and Latin America, caused sales of his album to skyrocket. The album remained forty weeks inside the British top ten and 218 weeks altogether, making it the 58th bestselling album in UK history with sales over 2.4 million. The song has become a karaoke classic worldwide.

In 1998, Williams released another huge hit, Millennium which became his first solo number one when it was released. The song sold over 400 thousand copies and was certified gold. The third single released "Strong" was rather more disappointing peaking at number 4 but this was followed by "She's the One" which became his second UK number one single.

However his next album was to possibly show the peak of his career and from then onwards he went downhill due to constant rumours and problems in his private life. He had another hugely successful album in 1999 with "Sing when you're winning" which spawned another number one hit single "Rock DJ". The song was inspired by William's mentor and UNICEF ambassador Ian Dury who had died recently. Despite this success, the song failed to break in the United States charts, but it did get some TV airplay in channels such as MTV and VH1. The song went on to win several awards, among them, "Best Song of 2000" at the MTV Europe Music Awards, "Best Single of the Year" at the BRIT Awards and an MTV Video Music Award for Best Special Effects, the single went on to sell over 600,000 copies in the UK alone, being certified Platinum. His second single from the album featured a huge collaboration with Kylie Minogue titled "Kids". The song only reached number two in the UK singles chart. He later collaborated with friend Jonathon Wilkes and Nicole

16 **TAKE THAT** back for good

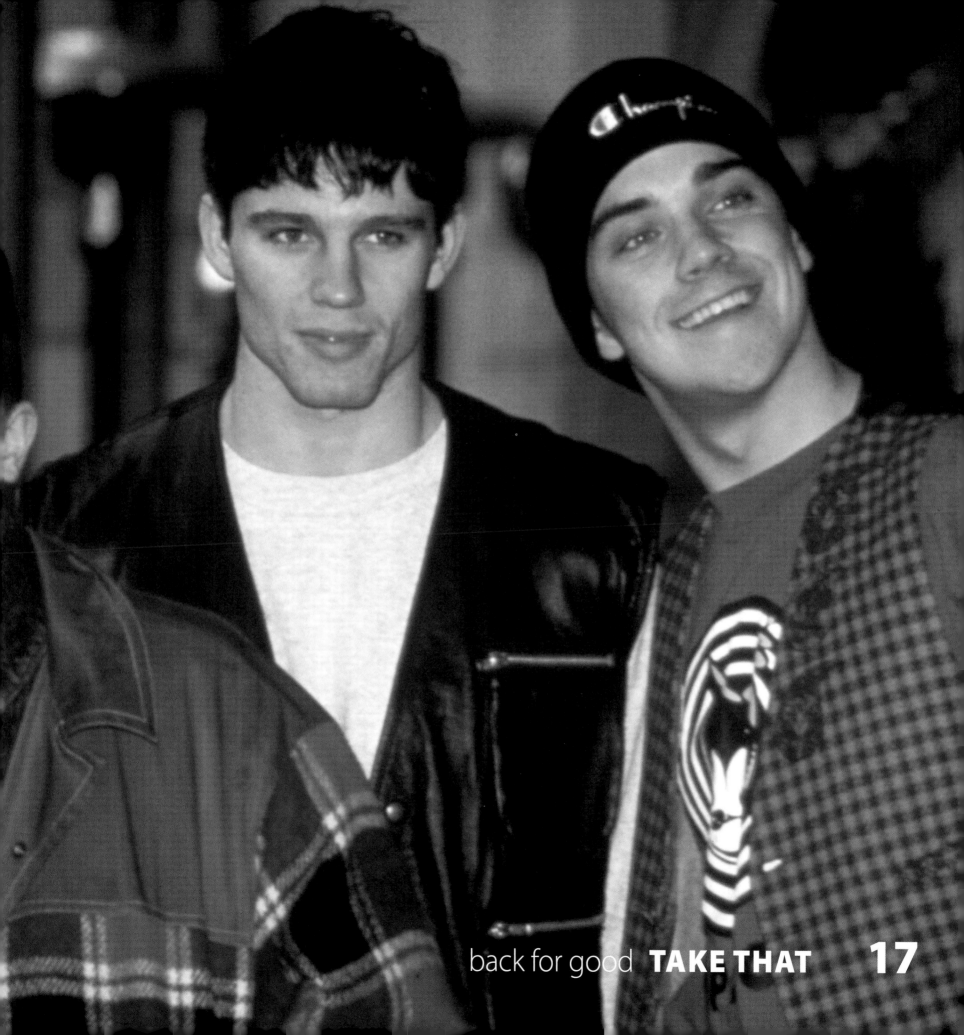

Kidman on a single called "Something Stupid" which became his fifth solo number one in the United Kingdom.

In 2003, Robbie Williams famously performed a series of live concerts and released a live album from Knebworth Park country house. The venue has become synonymous with live music and only highly respected and major artists play there. Previous acts before Williams' appearance had included Pink Floyd, The Rolling Stones, Oasis, Paul McCartney and Queen.

Robbie Williams performed at Knebworth over a three day period, drawing crowds of over 300,000 and a further 3.5 million who watched live on television and online. This was reputedly the biggest UK pop concert ever and caused a huge traffic jam on the A1 as an estimated 130,000 cars tried to reach the venue. A subsequent album, entitled "Robbie Williams – Live At Knebworth", was released, and reached number two in the UK charts. A DVD release followed.

The DVD released of that summer's three performances at Knebworth Park was entitled "What We Did Last Summer", a reference to the film I Know What You Did Last Summer. It went on to become the fastest selling music DVD in the United Kingdom selling 350,000 in total. Robbie's former Take That band mate Mark Owen was invited to perform Back For Good on stage with him at Knebworth. This was the first time the two had performed together since the band split in 1996. After performing with Robbie, Mark Owen returned to the spotlight signing a deal with Island/Universal Records. Owen himself was delighted to be reunited with Williams for the gig and it helped to launch his own solo career.

Robbie performed a set consisting of his solo material and some of Take That's more famous songs. The set over all 3 days would always open with "Let Me Entertain You" and close with "Angels", arguably two of the most well-known songs of the last decade and definitely Robbie's highest selling records. The only night that didn't finish with Angels was the opening night encore of Back for Good with Mark Owen. The actor Max Beesley appeared in all three performances with Williams to play percussion, despite now being a well-known actor himself.

After the gigs at Knebworth, he had further successes with albums such as "Escapology" and "Swing when you are winning" but none were anywhere near as successful as his previous solo work. In 2005 his single "Angels" was named as the Best British Single of the past twenty five years at The Brit Awards.

Williams's seventh studio album was announced in early 2006. It was to be a dance/electro album with collaborations with the Pet Shop Boys, William Orbit, Soul Mekanik, Joey Negro, Mark Ronson, Chris Grierson, The Orr Boys and more.

The first single, "Rudebox", was premièred on radio by Scott Mills on his show on BBC Radio 1. The event caused some controversy, as the record label's embargo date was broken, although the artist himself later backed the presenter for doing so. Right after the single was unleashed; it caused controversy due to Williams' radical change in direction from his other releases. British newspaper The Sun named the song "The Worst Song Ever". The single reached number four in the singles charts, failing to match the sales of the brand new reformed Take That. The second single, "Lovelight", came out right before the release of the album, and was commercially released on 13 November. The single reached the top ten in the United Kingdom but failed to reach the success of Williams's previous releases when the track showed no longevity in the charts.

The third single, "She's Madonna" reached only number sixteen on the Singles Chart in the United Kingdom, but fared better in Continental Europe hitting the top ten in most countries.

In 2009 after a quiet period he released the single "Bodies" on the Chris Moyles show on Radio 1. The DJ himself described the track as "one which grows on you with time". He caused controversy when he appeared to perform the track on the television show X Factor. The appearance proved to be somewhat controversial as press and viewers alike questioned Williams's well-being following a bizarre and erratic performance. A spokesperson for Williams later issued a public statement declaring that Williams had not been taking drugs. On 12 December 2009 Williams appeared again on the show to duet with finalist Olly Murs. Despite the claims Robbie missed his cue, he was unaware of the long instrumental and therefore began too early. However, after laughing it off and picking up his place again from Olly Murs, he managed to complete the performance without any other negative incidents.

The rumours began in 2010 that Williams and Barlow were going to duet together and possibly Williams would return to make Take That five again. This was announced in the summer and the two also decided to do a song together. They released the single Shame which made it to number 2 in the charts in October 2010. Since 2006, Williams has spent most of his time in Los Angeles, California and has commented many times on how he enjoyed the freedom and privacy because he is not so famous there. Williams moved back to the UK in 2009 when he bought an £8.5 million mansion in Compton

Bassett, Wiltshire, nearby to close friend Jonathan Wilkes who lives in Swindon. Williams sold the mansion a year later to move back to Los Angeles.

In 2010 Williams married his three year girlfriend Ayda Field in Los Angeles. She had helped him overcome his drug addictions in 2007 and had also forced him into giving up cigarettes. He proposed to her live on an Australian radio show in November 2009 just a few months after appearing on Jonathon Ross proclaiming his undying love for Field.

Williams is continuously involved in charity projects, most noticeably his charity football match featuring legendary players and celebrities. Started in 2006 the event has run every two years and been broadcast live on ITV. It raises money for UNICEF in the UK and has featured amongst others Diego Maradona, David Ginola, Ruud Gullit, Alan Shearer and Luis Figo. To date Williams has managed to raise over two and a half million pounds for UNICEF through Soccer Aid.

JASON ORANGE

Jason Orange's route into showbiz was rather different from the rest of the group. He started off as a backing dancer for several other groups before becoming well renowned for his breakdancing. He had joined the Manchester group "Street Machine Crew" before he was picked up by Take That to perform dance routines and as a mainly backing vocalist.

Orange was born in Crumpsall in Greater Manchester in 1970, and is like Gary Barlow a prolific songwriter who has also done some acting and television work between Take That splitting and reforming. Orange has five brothers (including a twin brother), as well as two half-sisters. Orange's family moved to the Wythenshawe area of South Manchester whilst he was a child. He attended Haveley Hey Primary School, and later attended South Manchester High School. He left school with no qualifications and went on a YTS scheme as an apprentice painter and decorator with Direct Works, the local council's repair and maintenance division.

As a youth, he was raised Mormon by his family, but they renounced the faith when he was a teenager. In an interview, Orange claimed that although he currently believes in God, "I'm still questioning religion." Jason Orange has no known girlfriend and has never married.

After Take That disbanded on 13 February 1996, Orange was the only group member who did not contemplate a solo career in music and instead tried his hand at acting. In 1998, he accompanied actor Max

Beesley, who had also played percussion on tour for the band, on a trip to New York where the pair both studied acting. As a result of the trip, Orange played a character called DJ Brent Moyer in the Lynda La Plante thriller Killer Net in 1998, which was shown on Channel 4. In 1999, he performed in the stage production Gob by Jim Kenworth at The King's Head Theatre in London. However, his ambitions to forge a career as an actor were ultimately unsuccessful and he gave up acting, stating that he could not stand the auditions.

Orange used his time away from Take That to do a large amount of travelling around Europe and Asia and also attended South Trafford College in Manchester where he studied for A Levels in Biology, History, Sociology and Psychology.

Jason Orange has only ever sung lead vocals for Take That on one track, the 2008 hit "How Did It Come To This" which features on the "Circus" album. However he has now taken to playing the guitar onstage during the band's tours after first picking up the instrument during the making of Take That's 1993 number one hit "Babe".

HOWARD DONALD

Howard Paul Donald was born in April 1968 in Droylsden, Lancashire. Donald is described as being a bit of a jack of all trades. He is a singer-songwriter, drummer, pianist, dancer, DJ and house producer. As well as working with Jason Orange as band choreographers, he sang lead vocals on one of the band's many number one singles first time round, "Never Forget". In addition, he also wrote and sang lead vocals of the song entitled "If This Is Love" from the band's album, Everything Changes.

Donald was educated at Moorside Primary School and Littlemoss High School. He is the father of two daughters, Grace and Lola from two separate relationships. His elder daughter Grace was born to Victoria Piddington, while he had his younger daughter with former girlfriend Marie-Christine Muss Wessels, the two split in the later half of 2009.

Donald was arguably one of the quieter and more reserved members of Take That similar to Jason Orange. Although Donald at first tried to pursue a solo career after Take That it proved to be a fruitless task and he had limited success from his solo singles. He recorded a single called "Speak Without Words" but unfortunately he couldn't find a record label to put

TAKE THAT back for good

the song out and it remains unreleased to this date.

After the failure of his solo career Donald decided that he would continue his passion for music and become more of a DJ as opposed to a vocalist. He is hugely popular in Europe and has even formed his own DJ band called Sonic Fly which features his friends King Brian and Bart Van Der Zwaan. He works under the name DJHD and has a fan base is Germany where he has become almost a household name in the dance music scene. Despite returning to Take That he has continued to DJ in Europe when he isn't on tour or promoting Take That songs.

Donald has had many publicised psychological problems between the split of Take That and the band's reformation including admitting in a public interview that he intended to kill himself. Donald said in the documentary Take That for the Record that "After the split I couldn't move on, so I intended to kill myself, I was going to commit suicide by drowning myself in the River Thames in London." Donald also admitted to previously having problems with drugs and that he had become depressed when Take That broke up and wasn't sure which direction to turn. In 2007 he caused further controversy when he admitted his support for the legalization of cannabis saying "If more people went out stoned than drunk I think there would be less fighting, less trouble, and less violence." He also admitted to having "dabbled with ecstasy" in the past.

He has also suffered from major health problems in recent years, notably in 2007 when during the Take That Beautiful World Tour he suffered a collapsed lung. Donald was performing an energetic dance routine and performing a series of gymnastic moves on stage at the time. He was kept in hospital for two days and the band had to perform as a threesome before he returned to continue the final leg of the tour.

MARK OWEN

Mark Owen was born in 1972 in Oldham, Lancashire. He lived in a small council house with his mother Mary, his father Keith, brother Daniel and sister Tracy. His father was a decorator, later getting a job at a police station and his mother was a supervisor in a bakery in Oldham.

Owen was educated at the Holy Rosary Primary and St Augustine's Catholic School in Oldham. Mark's first ambition was to be a professional footballer; he starred in school plays but showed no interest in music at school, preferring football. He played for Chadderton F.C. for a brief period. He also had trials for Manchester United, Huddersfield Town and Rochdale, but damaged his groin and was unable to pursue a career in the sport.

During the Take That "quiet" years, Owen spent some time back in Lancashire and was often spotted at musical events put on and performed by the local boarding school, "Casterton School". He used the school gymnasium on Tuesday evenings for football practice with friends.

After the breakup of Take That Owen decided that he too would try and pursue a solo career in music, and whilst not as successful as either Williams or Barlow, Owen proved that he could sing and did have some limited success as a soloist. He reached number three in the UK Singles Chart with his debut single, "Child" and his second single, "Clementine", also went to number three. However after his early successes the sales began to fade away. In 1997 his album Green Man was released, charting at number 33 and after another single, "I Am What I Am", charted at number 29, Owen was dropped by BMG Records in late 1997.

Owen then made the rather odd decision to step away from the limelight until making a spectacular comeback in 2002 when he appeared on the second series of Celebrity Big Brother and managed to win the entire competition. In the final public vote Owen received an astounding 77% of the vote, beating television presenter Les Dennis into second place. Both Dennis and Owen had bonded in the house and both had gone through extraordinary mental anguish with Les Dennis effectively suffering a mental breakdown. Owen broke down in tears when the result was announced saying that after the poor sales of some of his singles, he thought he didn't have any fans left from the Take That days. It highlighted the power of Take That's fans and Mark Owen's ability to win people round with his boyish charm.

After being invited to perform on stage with Robbie Williams at Knebworth, he returned to the spotlight and signed a deal with Island Records who were then owned by Universal. In August 2003, Owen returned to the charts with the Top 5 hit, "Four Minute Warning", which remained in the charts for eight weeks but after a second single, "Alone Without You", charted at number 26, Owen was dropped by his record label.

In April 2004 he established his own record company, Sedna Records but he was plagued by allegations of bankruptcy, One report around 2004 even alleged that Owen was looking for a day job to get money, but he simply said "Doing it properly isn't cheap. These are my indulgences. I don't have a Ferrari, I have two albums." Mark Owen has repeatedly vowed to continue in music even after Take That disband again and says he wants to form his own group in the future.

Owen has suffered from drink problems throughout recent years. In March of 2010, he checked himself into a rehabilitation clinic in order to overcome an alcohol addiction. In 2006 Mark Owen became engaged to actress Emma Ferguson. The pair married in 2009 and they have two children called Elwood and Willow Rose.

In recent times the marriage has been dogged by repeated allegations of infidelity on the part of Owen who admitted to sleeping with as many as ten other women whilst with his wife. He blamed his actions on his drink problem, saying it caused him to become depressed and desperate. At the time of the revelations Owen revealed how he felt he had totally let down his fans and his wife "I denied to her I was having an affair when things were going on. We met and within a year and a half she was pregnant with our first beautiful boy, Elwood. And when you have kids, things change. I feel like I am getting to know Em more and more every day. I love her to death but our relationship hasn't always been great, because of me. Life was hard, I guess. I let Emma down. I was selfish and stubborn."

Despite the constant media speculation, the pair managed to overcome the difficulties and Owen has managed to rebuild his private life.

The origins of Take That
1989-1992

In 1989, Nigel Martin-Smith sought to create a British male vocal singing group. Martin-Smith was a Manchester based music producer and manager who at the time was working in Manchester's Royal Exchange. In the early 1990s, following the success of US boy band New Kids on the Block, Martin-Smith decided to create a British version of New Kids On The Block with a similar "chosen" formula of singers and dancers.

back for good **TAKE THAT** 27

Martin-Smith's vision, however, was more teen-oriented than the clean-cut image that the New Kids sported in the media. A campaign to audition young men with abilities in dancing and singing took place in Manchester and other surrounding cities in 1990. Martin-Smith met budding songwriter Gary Barlow through an agent friend, whom Barlow had hired to take professional head shots. Impressed with Barlow's catalogue of self-written material, he put him into the group. At twenty-two, Howard Donald was one of the oldest to audition, but he managed to become accepted into the band after getting off work as a vehicle painter. When asked to recruit other possible candidates, Donald recommended fellow street dancer Jason Orange, who had appeared as a dancer on The Hitman and Her. Mark Owen and Robbie Williams met on the day of their audition and interview.

Nigel Martin-Smith's original suggestion for the name of the band was Kick It but the members of the band claimed they did not like it. Gary Barlow has stated that the name of Take That was the "worst of a bad bunch, suggested by Nigel." Barlow actually suggested calling themselves "The English" something which would later reappear in 2010 when Robbie Williams re-joined the group. In 2010 Barlow said the band should reform for a couple of singles with Robbie so that they could re-establish themselves with Robbie's musical style.

Take That's first TV appearance was on The Hitman & Her in 1990, where they performed the unreleased songs "Love" and "My Kind of Girl." They later appeared a second time to perform "Waiting Around", which would become the B-side for the first single, "Do What U Like". "Promises" and "Once You've Tasted Love" were also released as singles but were minor hits in the UK. The band's breakthrough single was a cover of the 1970s Tavares hit "It Only Takes a Minute", which peaked at number 7 on the UK Singles Chart. This success was followed by the track "I Found Heaven", then by the first Barlow ballad "A Million Love Songs" both top 20 hits.

Their cover of the Barry Manilow disco hit "Could It Be Magic" gave them their biggest hit to date, peaking at number 3 in the UK. To this day Could It Be Magic remains one of the fans' favourite songs and a staple of both the disco and karaoke scene. The decision by the group to cover this song was inspired as the public related to a song they already knew and acknowledged the new pop genre that the band were trying to create.

Their first album was called Take That and Party and was released in 1991 featuring a compilation of their greatest hits to date. Take That and Party became an instant success and started to establish the group on a worldwide stage. It reached number two in the UK album chart, showing the public had an appetite for this new style of popular music. The band had established themselves by writing their own lyrics but also by reworking classic 70s and 80s pop songs. Most of the songs on the album were written by Gary Barlow who had already established himself as the band leader, something which would later lead to problems with the ego of both Barlow and Williams who would become the public favourite. The album featured some of the group's most famous songs including "Promises", "A Million love songs", "Could it be Magic" and "It only takes a minute". All of these songs still feature regularly on radio playlists and on the band's own live sets.

The question would become, were Take That merely a one hit wonder or could they release a follow up album that was even more successful than their debut. The answer would become clear a couple of years later with the release of the album "Everything Changes".

The superstar band
1992-1995

In 1992 and 1993 the band continued to grow, attracting fans from a wider variety of age groups both young and old. The band was approaching the release of their second album, which can often prove the death of many a new band. They released the album Everything Changes which spawned a series of top ten hits.

The album itself was released in 1993 and entirely based on Barlow's original material. It became the first album which didn't feature songs written by other artists such as Barry Manilow. It spawned four UK number one singles – their first number one "Pray", "Relight My Fire", "Babe", which was quite amazingly beaten to the Christmas number one stop by Mr Blobby, and the title track "Everything Changes". The fifth single "Love Ain't Here Anymore" reached number three in the UK charts. Everything Changes saw the band gain international success, but it failed to crack the US market where an exclusive remix of the song "Love Ain't Here Anymore" gained little success. Everything Changes reached number one in the UK album chart and was nominated for the 1994 Mercury Music Prize, The album was certified platinum four times over which means it sold millions of copies in the UK and worldwide. It also reached the top 10 in Ireland, Austria, Holland, Germany, Hungary, Belgium and Switzerland.

The album itself received rave reviews worldwide getting four and a half stars from All-music, the reviewers of the album said "By this time they were giant superstars in Europe, and the question in their minds was not whether they could get a hit single, but how many and which would make it to number one. The album spawned six hit singles, four of which made number one, making it Record of the Year and one of the best-selling albums of the decade, proclaiming them the biggest male group since the Beatles. When the hype sets in, it is hard to distinguish the value of the material itself. It is an album of dance-pop and ballads sung by five young men, with a greater maturity than most boy band albums thanks to the writing by lead singer. Boy bands have their share of sceptics, and getting those to tear down their defences usually ends up competing with their struggle to please the fan base they already have. Through the album, Take That won over everyone they needed to. What they got in return was a reputation for being a fine group with real talent. Everything Changes marked the height of Take That's worldwide popularity.

In 1993 the band went on their first ever nationwide tour in order to promote the Everything Changes album. They had played smaller venue tours in 1992, for the Take That and Party Tour but this was recognised as their first serious group tour. They started in 1993 with the UK Summer Tour playing Wembley Arena for the first time as well as Manchester, Glasgow, Birmingham and Chelmsford. Later in 1993, they embarked on their biggest tour to date. The tour was known as the "Everything Changes Tour" and featured songs from the first

TAKE THAT back for good

album and some new and as yet unreleased material. The tour lasted almost a month with the band playing 3 or 4 gigs a week. They also left the mainland for the first time travelling to Belfast and Dublin. In addition to those they played Bournemouth, Cardiff, Birmingham, Brighton, Wembley in London, Manchester, Sheffield, Glasgow, Aberdeen and rather oddly closed the tour at Whitley Bay's Ice Rink.

By 1994, the band had become radio and television stars across Europe and Asia. In 1995 the band embarked on their first ever World Tour, taking in Europe and Asia, where the band had become international superstars. Between 1992 and 1995, the band began to take over the front cover of hundreds of magazines ranging from Smash Hits to GQ, becoming mass merchandised on all sorts of paraphernalia ranging from picture books, to posters, stickers, their own dolls, jewellery, caps, T-shirts, toothbrushes and even had their own annuals released. However despite their raised media profile and marketability, the group never managed to crack the lucrative American market.

The band had also developed a large female teenage fan base at the time. During this time, they performed at numerous music awards shows and chart shows such as the BRIT Awards and Top of the Pops, also winning the Best Live Act award in

1995 at the MTV Europe Music Awards, having been renowned for their breakdance routines, melodious harmonies, elaborate costumes and flamboyant stage props.

In 1995 Take That released their 3rd studio album Nobody Else, again based on Barlow's own material. It was to be their last album released before the breakup in 1996. The album spawned three number 1 singles: "Sure", "Back for Good" and "Never Forget". The single release of Never Forget in July 1995 marked the departure of Robbie Williams, who had decided that he wanted to pursue his own solo career. The album reached number one in the UK, German, Dutch and Swiss charts and was also released in America with a different track listing containing many of their previous singles. In support of the album, the band went on the Nobody Else Tour, playing 31 dates across countries such as the UK, Australia, Thailand, Singapore and Japan. The album has been certified as double Platinum in the UK. The album was also noted for its cover which was a parody of the famed cover of The Beatles' Sgt. Pepper's Lonely Hearts Club Band cover sleeve.

The release of "Sure", their first single from the album, achieved yet another number one in the UK Charts. It was not until their second release from that album however, that they would experience what would become their biggest hit single, "Back for Good".

The single "Back for Good" is one of the fastest selling and highest grossing records of the entire decade. It is also arguably Take That's most well-known and memorable song from the original period of the band. Written by Gary Barlow, who also sang the lead vocal on the track, it was their sixth UK chart-topper, and their only US top ten hit. It was initially unveiled at the 1995 BRIT Awards, and such was the demand for the single that the release date was brought forward and the song made available to the media an unprecedented six weeks before release. It was released on March 27, 1995 and entered the UK singles chart at number one, selling nearly 350,000 copies in its first week and selling almost as many as the rest of the top 10 that week added together. It remained at number one for four weeks. It is the group's biggest selling single in the UK, with sales reaching over a million by 2010. The song has since appeared on most album releases and covers that the group have put out, albeit in a slightly remixed form, which added some extra instrumentation including additional drum beats.

The song won Best British Single at the 1996 Brit Awards. The song would later reach number seven on the American Billboard Hot 100 chart. The song was also a big hit in Brazil, during the years of 1995 and 1996, due to soap-opera "Explode Coração" on which the song appeared as one of the main songs on the TV show's soundtrack. Robbie Williams would later record his own version of the song as a B-side to his monster smash hit "Angels" released in 1998.

The song has featured in numerous television programmes and has been covered by tens of artists worldwide. It was featured on the final episode of the second series of "Spaced", and also featured in the final episode of Ricky Gervais and Stephen Merchant's The Office as a love theme for characters Tim who was played by Martin Freeman and Dawn played by Lucy Davis.

Gary Barlow stated on ITV1's An Audience with Take That Live broadcast on 2 December 2006 that there were 89 recorded versions of the song by other artists. The song has received a Platinum sales status certification in the UK. "Back for Good" was covered by Boyz II Men for their Love album. Coldplay performed this song with Gary Barlow at Shepherd's Bush Empire, London in aid of War Child in 2009.

The band also shot and released a music video for "Back for Good" something which the band hadn't done with many of their other singles and perhaps highlighting the overwhelming success of both the song and the band at this time in their careers.

The video was shot in black and white. The group at the start are running through the rain and into a hut. Jason is playing the guitar and the others are sitting around singing the song. Towards the end of the video the group sing the song and dance in the rain, with the cars, a 1958 Chevrolet Impala and a 1951 Mercury both featured in the background and customised to fit the 1950s style of the video.

After Robbie - the breakup 1995-1996

After the successful release of the Nobody Else album the band began a long worldwide tour in order to promote themselves as a group and to enhance their worldwide media image. This proved to be the beginning of the end for the band as a five part group. Despite their newfound fame all was not well in the relationship between the band's individual parts.

back for good **TAKE THAT** | **39**

Wenn

Howard, Jason and Mark felt that they weren't being totally appreciated, as did Gary who felt that Robbie was hogging the limelight undeservedly, after all it was Gary who was responsible for actually writing the hits. The fans however were beginning to view the group as Robbie Williams and four backing vocalists.

The months between June of 1995 and February of 1996 were destined to be the most turbulent and troubled of Take That's career and also would shape some of the problems of their later solo careers. Robbie Williams had spiralled out of control and had begun to take drugs and drink heavily. He was becoming addicted to hard substances and this was affecting his performances particularly during the staging of the tour to promote the Nobody Else album. Gary Barlow meanwhile was beginning to grow disillusioned with the rest of the band and felt that his writing talent should be more recognised. The rest of the group weren't overly pleased with Robbie's perceived image of himself as the new band leader and things started to come to a head.

In July 1995, Robbie Williams' drug abuse had escalated to a near drug overdose the night before the group was scheduled to perform at the MTV Europe Music Awards. According to the documentary For the Record, Williams was unhappy with his musical ideas not being taken seriously by lead singer Barlow and

Nigel Martin-Smith, because his desires to explore more hip hop and the rap genre conflicted with the band's usual ballads. Barlow explained in interviews that Williams had given up trying to offer creative input and merely did as he was told. As well as the friction with Nigel, Jason had problems with Robbie's increasingly belligerent behaviour and his habit of missing the band's rehearsals. Both he and Barlow confronted Martin-Smith about the internal conflict, because they did not want Robbie dropping out while touring and before they planned to explore America in the next few years, which ultimately never came to pass. During one of the last rehearsals before the tour commenced, they confronted Robbie about his attitude and stated they wanted to do the tour without him. He agreed to quit the band and left; it would be the last time for twelve years that they were all together. Shortly afterwards, Williams was photographed by the press partying with fellow band Oasis at Glastonbury Festival. Following his departure, he became the subject of talk shows and newspapers as he acknowledged his plans to become a solo singer, and he was spotted partying with George Michael in France.

However, a clause in his Take That contract prohibited him from releasing any material until after the group was officially dissolved, and he was later sued by Nigel and forced to pay almost 200 thousand pounds in compensation.

In 1995 the band went on their first ever "World Tour" designed to promote both themselves as a band and also the latest album. The plan was to try and expand the band into worldwide stars by touring Australia, Japan, Singapore, Thailand and Korea. It formed part of the "Nobody Else Tour" which became known by the fans as the first tour the band ever did without Robbie Williams present. The remaining four started off in Manchester and London before eventually moving on to Asia and Australia, but things had suddenly changed and the band's attitude to music had stretched their friendships to breaking point. The tour featured a compilation of some of Take That's finest work and greatest hits to that point always beginning with "Relight My Fire" and ending with "Never Forget". The Earls Court concerts in London were recorded for a VHS release entitled "Nobody Else the movie", the video also contained some bonus promotional footage of the band practising and of three songs "Sure", "Back for Good" and "Never Forget".

Perhaps this article written for The Daily Telegraph sums up some of the fans opinions about the departure of Robbie Williams and the general feeling that the band will be far better off without him: "Take That don't need Robbie. He doesn't need them. It will only end in tears, again. Besides, there are the girls to consider, those who cried inconsolably on the day in 1995 when the band said they were going their separate ways. They will feel cheated. And it won't just be the girls. A friend of mine – a pillar of the community now – was decorating his sitting room when the news came on the radio. He admits that he started crying, too – though he did have a hangover at the time and was "feeling fragile". Some bands are just not meant to reform. They occupy a moment in our cultural history that cannot be reclaimed."

Undaunted by the loss of Robbie Williams, Take That continued to promote Nobody Else as a four piece, scoring a further hit single with Barlow's "Never Forget" and completing the Nobody Else Tour in July 1995. However it became clear to some people that the group had begun to lose their unique passion and regardless of what Gary Barlow thought, some critics argued they had lost their frontman. On 13 February 1996, Take That formally announced that they were disbanding. This decision was followed by the release of a Greatest Hits compilation in 1996, which contained a new recording, a cover of The Bee Gees' "How Deep Is Your Love". The single went on to become what was to be the band's final UK number one until their 2006 comeback a decade later. Take That gave what was then thought to be their final performance in April 1996 at Amsterdam.

The band's decision to separate sent shockwaves around the world and almost overnight they became headline news with many people totally shocked and overwhelmed by the band's sudden departure from music. In an indication of the band's global fame and hardcore following of fans there was a mass outcry and even people threatening to commit suicide following the split. Immediately after the band's announcement, millions of their fans were distraught around the world and in the UK alone, teenage girls threatened suicide or self-harm and were seen lining streets in tears, to the point that telephone hotlines were set up by the government to deal with counselling them. Some fans even held candlelit vigils in the streets of their home towns with pictures of the four remaining members praying for the group to reunite. There were numerous campaigns on television and through telephones and children's television to try and reunite the band and persuade them to change their mind. The impact of Take That's demise brought about a new era in pop music where girl bands and cheesy classics were reaching number one. However, many of Take That's fans never got over the group being disband and to this day haven't forgiven the band and will not buy any of their new music.

Take That had left the music industry on a high

unlike so many bands who keeping putting out records until nobody is buying them anymore. That is the fundamental reason that the group managed to maintain their fan base through the following ten years as I will go on to discuss in the next chapter. The group had spawned so many successful hits that even the BBC news at ten ran with the story of the group's break up. The story continued to roll for the next 10 years.

Between 1996 and 2006 what happened to the fans?

Some of the fans involved in Take That throughout their meteoric rise in the 1990s never got over the group's decision to split. They were Take That loyalists, with no intention of following the boys' solo careers or indeed in some cases continuing to live without the group's music in their lives. However for ten years there was no new release from the group and the die-hard fans had to preoccupy themselves with the occasional rumour of a possible reunion for an album without Robbie or the occasional television appearance. So how did a band whose music career to this date had only spanned six years manage to remain in the minds of millions of fans and still on the playlists of many top music channels and radio stations in the UK and Worldwide?

Well firstly there was the rise of the internet as a global necessity where everyone could share their thoughts and hundreds of websites entirely dedicated to the band's music, history and style were introduced. Many of the websites also had online discussion forums which would allow fans to discuss everything about the band ranging from their favourite song, to the best singer and even which of the boys in Take That was "the fittest". Some of these websites claim to have over a million members of which at least two hundred thousand are regularly active and in some way involved on the site.

One fan site called the Take That appreciation pages was set up on the 1st April 1996 just two months after the band split up and has been running constantly ever since. They greet visitors to the website by saying "Take That Appreciation Pages has been running since 1st April 1996, and is dedicated to Thatters all over the world! We are an unofficial website, run by fans for fans who will Never Forget the genius that will always be Take That! We were deeply saddened when the boys split and were delighted by the reunion in 2005 and hope they will continue to make the music we love to hear." The site itself has had over 2.6 million viewers since they started in 1996 and is regarded as one of the finest unofficial fan sites for any group in the world.

Perhaps it could be argued that the band remained iconic and significant because of their radio and television airplay throughout the decade between

back for good **TAKE THAT** **45**

1996 and 2006. The band still managed to dominate radio playlists and request shows, even without releasing any new records. Songs such as Relight My Fire and Back for Good were used in movies, television adverts and often picked as first dance songs by romantic couple who had lived through the Take That era for their wedding. Through the fans that had grown up with the group and who had now become the music makers and DJs themselves, the band remained in the forefront of people's minds.

They also survived thanks to a high level of media interest in the group and constant stories about the band members and also alleged reunions being printed almost weekly throughout the late 90s and mid-2000s. The solo artists often used these reunion rumours to highlight their own solo careers and say how they were doing fine without the group. However it was widely acknowledged and accepted that Gary Barlow, Jason Orange, Howard Donald and Mark Owen had remained fairly close throughout their solo careers and that only Robbie Williams had been isolated. The band also thrived on the constant rumours surrounding their private lives and sexual preferences. For example Mark Owen was hounded in both the 90s and more recently since the reformation by rumours and stories of alleged infidelity. Owen himself later admitted some infidelity but managed to save his marriage and came

out stronger as a result. Williams was also hounded by the paparazzi who were fully aware of his drink and drug problems. They tried to catch him at his worst moments but despite this his fans and fans of Take That as a whole stayed loyal and hoped that in the long run the band might be reunited.

The band maintained a media profile through public appearances like Mark Owen in Celebrity Big Brother and Gary Barlow's involvement in charity work. Barlow occasionally was spotted eating out with Howard Donald and Jason Orange. Mark Owen had kept in touch with Robbie Williams since 1995 and as well as performing at Knebworth with Williams, occasionally spoke on the phone. Despite some members of the band having obvious differences of opinion, they managed to maintain contact with one another throughout the ten years. It was as a result of this they were able to patch up any differences in 2005 and reunite in time for the 2006 album release.

However what we can conclude is that despite releasing no new material for ten years, Take That had remained in the public limelight throughout their absence because the public had craved their return. When it finally did happen in 2006, the hype that once again surrounded the band was almost the exact opposite of the sadness that had befallen the nation in 1996.

The return of the band and Beautiful World 2006-2008

In 2005 strong rumours began to appear in the papers that the band had started to meet up and were secretly recording material. The rumours got stronger when Gary Barlow and Mark Owen were spotted in Los Angeles outside a recording studio that Barlow had used previously.

TAKE THAT back for good

The speculation grew that the band were planning to do a comeback tour and possibly even reform for a new album to celebrate both the greatest hits from the 90s and new material written by Barlow.

On 14 November 2005, "Never Forget The Ultimate Collection", a new compilation of their hit singles including a new previously unreleased song, also achieved great success and peaked at #2 in the UK charts. The new song "Today I've Lost You" which was recorded by the band in Los Angeles in 2005, was originally written by Gary Barlow as the follow up to "Back for Good" but was never recorded. On 16 November 2005, the group of four that finished the band in 1996, got back together for the ITV documentary Take That: For the Record, in which they aired their views over the split and what they had been up to during the last 10 years.

On 25 November 2005, there was an official press conference by the band announcing that the post Robbie Williams line-up were going to tour in 2006. This report featured in the Guardian in November shortly after the band had held the press conference:

"When the four remaining members of Take That last appeared on stage together a decade ago, they had to fight through a throng of weeping teenage fans. But as they announced their return yesterday, just three diehards braved the cold to welcome them back, if not quite for good, then long enough to go on a money spinning nostalgia tour next spring.

Robbie Williams, who walked out on the band six months before they split in 1996, will not take part. But the other four Gary Barlow, Jason Orange, Howard Donald and Mark Owen said their former bandmate had given them his "blessing" and they were looking forward to playing to their old fans who have taken their current greatest hits album to number two in the charts.

Walking into a press conference to the strains of Back For Good the band, who sold 9m albums and 10m singles between 1992 and 1996 and paved the way for a host of imitators, said that they had discussed the idea after reuniting to promote a recent ITV documentary.

Barlow, who wrote many of their hits but whose own solo career faltered, said that they weren't getting any younger, so it was "now or never". The absence of Williams hung heavily over proceedings, with Barlow admitting they would have "loved" it if he was involved."

At the press conference they announced more of the details of the tour which would comprise 11 tour dates and reportedly could net each of the group a million pounds. Jason Orange joked that "based on the fact I'm currently doing nowt, the money will come in handy"

The tour, entitled Ultimate Tour, ran from April to June 2006. It featured two nights at the Wembley Stadium and a total of 32 shows throughout its run. The tour mainly focused on big cities with shows being held in Birmingham, Manchester, Newcastle, Sheffield, Glasgow, Dublin and Belfast. The Ultimate Tour was the first time that Take That had performed together since they split in 1996. It featured a guest appearance by British soul singer Beverley Knight, who replaced Lulu's vocals on the song "Relight My Fire"; although Lulu did appear during the stadium shows on "Relight My Fire" and "Never Forget". The American female ensemble Pussycat Dolls supported the group at their Dublin concert, and the Sugababes supported the group on the final five dates of the stadium leg. The tickets for the two gigs at Wembley Stadium sold out inside 30 minutes and in total on the day of opening, the band sold 275 thousand tickets in 3 hours.

After the successes of the tour, the band announced that they would perform further dates as part of what they called Stage 2 of the Ultimate Tour. They added dates in Milton Keynes and Dublin as well as at the City of Manchester Stadium and The Millennium Stadium in Cardiff.

Then came the moment that fans had been waiting almost a decade for, on the 9th of May 2006, Take That came back to the recorded music scene after more than ten years, signing with Polydor Records in a deal reportedly worth 3 million pounds. The band's comeback album, Beautiful World, entered the UK album chart at number one 1 and by 2010 had sold almost three million copies in the UK. It is currently the 35th best-selling album in UK music history. The week after Take That's comeback album Beautiful World was released it was announced that Take That had become the first artists ever to top the UK official single and album charts along with the download single, download album and DVD charts in the same week, as well as topping the radio charts.

On the album Beautiful World all four members of the band had the opportunity to sing lead vocals. Unlike the band's earlier works, where the majority of their material was written by Gary Barlow who received a sole credit, all four band members are credited as co-writers, regardless of whether they contributed to the writing process or not. The comeback single, "Patience", was released in November 2006, with a special event launching it on 5 November, to tie in with Bonfire Night. On Sunday the 26th of November "Patience" hit number 1 in the UK in its second week of chart entry making it the group's ninth number one and their first for ten years. The single managed to stay at number one for 4 weeks. In a sign of their return to the mainstream music scene, Take That accompanied Leona Lewis in a version of "A Million Love Songs" in the final of The X Factor in December 2006, just before she went on to win the show.

Take That themselves described the "Beautiful World" album as "a throwback to the 1990s, and to an era and musical style which boy bands had now deserted". Despite only being on sale for one month of 2006, it became the second highest album of the entire year and has been certified platinum no less than 8 times. The album also became the first one to feature all of the group's members on vocals and they were also all involved in both the choreography and lyrics.

Critics were unanimous in their praise of the album. "The album doesn't try for anything too dramatic and oozes with their obvious joy and gratitude at being back at the top of their game. Hearing Gary's voice on the majority of the tracks is a comforting reminder of times past, but having the other three as lead singers provides a refreshing change, with Jason Orange's Wooden Boat standing out particularly. The songs are varied and more reflective than their previous work evoking the struggles to stick together and time passing. Their amazing comeback single

'Patience' jostles for prominence amongst a string of epic opening tracks including 'Reach Out' and 'Hold On'. Then there are the beautiful ballads 'Like I've Never Loved You At All', stand out track 'I'd Wait For Life' and the pensive 'What You Believe In'. The album gets its really interesting twist with the Beatles-esque 'Shine' and the folk-tinged 'Wooden Boat'."

The second single, "Shine" was released in February 2007 shortly before the band was nominated for more BRIT Awards. It immediately went to number one in the UK singles chart. The band's success continued on 14 February 2007 when Take That performed live at the BRIT Awards ceremony at Earl's Court. Their single "Patience" won the Best British Single category. The third single taken from Beautiful World was "I'd Wait For Life", released on 18 June 2007 in the UK. However the single only reached 17 in the UK Singles Chart, falling out of the top 40 the following week. This was due to lack of promotion, as the band decided to take a pre-tour break rather than do any promotion for the single.

During 2007, Take That also wrote a song for the motion picture Stardust titled "Rule the World", which reached number 2 in the UK charts and went on to be the 5th biggest selling single of 2007. Meanwhile, the album Beautiful World was the fourth biggest-selling album of 2007. It was announced at the start of 2007

back for good **TAKE THAT** | **53**

Wenn

TAKE THAT *back for good*

back for good **TAKE THAT** | **57**

58 **TAKE THAT** back for good

Wenn

TAKE THAT back for good

TAKE THAT back for good

that Take That signed a record deal with American label Interscope Records.

Take That began their Beautiful World Tour 2007 in Belfast. The tour included 49 shows throughout Europe and the UK and ended in Manchester on 23 December 2007. For the first time the band visited countries outside of the UK and Ireland, including Germany, Austria, Spain, Italy, Switzerland, Denmark and Holland. The Beautiful World Tour garnered positive reviews from critics, and is to date their highest selling tour and one of the biggest tours in UK history. Sophie Ellis-Bextor was present at all UK dates as the special guest, except the 31 December gig at The O2 Arena, which was advertised as Countdown to Midnight: Take That & Sugababes. Each night a member of Take That chose an unsigned band/artist to support. The show itself including the staging and choreography cost about 4 million pounds to produce.

It was during this tour that the band went down to three members at one point. As I mentioned previously in the profile on Howard Donald, he managed to puncture his lung doing a stage jump in Vienna. During the routine for "Sure" he jumped and landed badly before hearing a crack. He later appeared on the tour in a hospital gown and even flashed his backside to the adoring fans. Donald re-joined the band for the Oberhausen gig in Germany.

In the aftermath of the 2007 tour the band received even more good news to start 2008. The band received four nominations at the 2008 BRIT Awards. They were nominated for Best British Group, Best British Single for "Shine", Best British Album for "Beautiful World" and Best Live Act. However despite receiving four nominations they only managed to win two for Best Live Act and Best British Single.

The release of Circus and the Tours 2008-2009

The latter half of 2008 saw Take That start to write new material for an album which they announced would be released in time for Christmas. The album was weirdly released exactly the same time as a Britney Spears album which shared the title "Circus". Take That's manager claimed the band had been working on the title for months and that they would not be changing it.

The biggest song from the album was also the first single the band chose to release. They chose "Greatest Day" as they felt it would connect with a wide section of people. The song went to number one in November 2008.

An album launch party for The Circus was held in Paris on the 2 December. Prior to the official release of the album, it was revealed that the band had broken all pre-order records and had become the most pre-ordered album of all time. On its first day of release The Circus sold 133,000 copies, and after four days on sale it sold 306,000 copies making The Circus the fastest selling album of the year. The album was also certified platinum by the end of its first week of sales. "The Circus" reached number 1 in the UK album charts in December 2008 with total first-week sales of just over 430 thousand, the third highest opening sales week in UK history.

The album itself received universally glowing views from the critics with its lowest review from a mainstream publication being 3 stars out of a possible 5. BBC Music said: "A stunning album, Take That are the vintage champagne of pop fizzing with playful bubbles and happily maturing with age". Sunday Mercury said: "Like its predecessor, The Circus boasts one killer track. Hit single Greatest Day is as pop-perfect now as Patience was back in 2006. Orange Music said: "An album of measured, mature songwriting by all four, it is by far their best". The Times said "Take That's 2009 return is the gold standard: a hugely successful second coming from a band determined not to fritter away their reserves of goodwill."

The first single released from the band was to be "Greatest Day" which critics were already raving about. It was debuted on Radio 1 in mid-October and became one of the classic pop records of all times. Major companies had decided to use it for adverts and it became the music of choice for journalists wanting to do an upbeat story and looking for music to match. "Greatest Day" was written by Gary Barlow and was recorded in Notting Hill before being mixed in Los Angeles where most of the band were based. It was at the Los Angeles recording studio where Jim Henson recorded the Muppets and also the famous reunion between Barlow and Robbie Williams. Take That performed the song at the MTV Europe Music Awards 2008 on 6 November 2008, the first pan-European live performance by the band, preceding the single's release on 24 November 2008. The song has sold 292,305 copies in the UK so far and has been certified Silver by the UK Charts Company. It was to become the band's 11th UK number one single. The song has since been used in numerous television programmes and ad campaigns. At the time the press made a huge amount out of Gary and Robbie's possible reunion and this helped the promotion of the single.

The Daily Mail featured a picture of Williams and Barlow outside the Los Angeles studio with this accompanying article. "Could this be the moment that Take That fans have been hoping for? Lead singer Gary Barlow sparked rumours that the entire band could soon be reunited after he was spotted outside a studio with Robbie Williams. According to reports, the pair had been recording together at the studio in Hollywood, California. Gary, 39, was snapped soaking up the sun outside the studio as he waited for Robbie, 36, to leave after they spent three hours inside."

In October 2008, on the Radio 1 Chris Moyles show, it was announced that Take That would be touring again in June and July 2009, covering England, Scotland and Wales. Tickets for the Take That Present: The Circus Live tour went on sale on 31 October and sold out within hours. The tour was recognised by the Guinness Book of Record for being the Fastest Selling UK Tour of all time.

On 22 May 2008, Barlow and Donald attended the 2008 Ivor Novello Awards where Take That won the award for Most Performed Work with their single "Shine". Take That won the Sony Ericsson Tour of the Year award at the Vodafone music awards on 18 September 2008. They were unable to attend as they were in LA finishing off The Circus, however the band did send a video link message, which was shown at the awards. In November the band appeared on the TV show X Factor, their second appearance in two years. They were on the show as part of a themed night where the finalists performed some of their greatest hits.

The band also performed on Children in Need 2008, singing their new single, "Greatest Day", before donating £250,000 to the charity from their Marks and Spencer fee. The band was also voted the Greatest Boy band of All Time, reflecting their on-going marketability and success in the pop arena, even after two decades.

2009 continued to be a successful year for the band when they were nominated for the BRITS and also asked to perform a song at the ceremony. They were nominated in the category of Best Group and performed "Greatest Day".

However after the successes of "Greatest Day", the rest of the single releases from the album failed to impress on the singles charts. "Up All Night", the second single from The Circus, was released in March 2009, and peaked at number 14 in the UK

Singles Chart, despite heavy airplay. In Germany and Australia, "The Garden" was released as the second single instead.

In May 2009, Take That's official website confirmed that the third single from The Circus would be "Said It All" which was released in June 2009, peaking at number 9 on the UK Singles chart. However by this point the band had turned their focus to the upcoming tour which would be titled "The Circus Live". They even produced a promotional music video for "Said it All" which features all four band members dressed up as vintage circus clowns, to promote tour sales.

The band had numerous special guests throughout the tour, The Script were the special guests at their gig at Croke Park in Dublin and the Sugababes and other smaller local bands also guested alongside Take That. The group also presented their own TV show Take That Come To Town, a variety show where they performed some of their biggest hits and new material from The Circus, which aired on December 7, 2008 on ITV.

On the 5th of June, the group began the tour at the Stadium of Light in Sunderland, and ended a month later at Wembley Stadium in London on the 5 July 2009. The Wembley gig was attended by well over 80 thousand people. This tour quickly became the fastest-selling of all time, breaking all records by selling all of their 650,000 tickets in less than four and a half hours. The tour became the fastest selling tour in UK history selling £35m of tickets in one day beating the previous record set by Michael Jackson for his Bad World Tour in 1987 though Jackson reclaimed the record soon after when he announced his residency at the O2 Arena in London shortly before his death. The tour also visited Coventry, Dublin, Cardiff, Glasgow and Manchester. The set list for the concerts began with a song called "The Adventures of a Lonely Balloon" from the new album and finished with the classic track "Rule the World".

The Live Tour in turn brought about the band's first ever live album recorded on stage at a Wembley gig from the tour. It featured a compilation of the live version of Take That's set and featured some of Take That's hits from the last 15 years. The album also included a bonus set of tracks recorded at the famous Abbey Road Studios.

The Circus Live sold 98,000 copies on its first day of release. This was roughly 35,000 copies below the first-day sales of their previous album, "The Circus". The album peaked at #3 in the UK Albums Chart, and was certified Platinum in December 2009. In order to promote the live album the band released "Hold up a Light" as the fifth and final single from The Circus. They promoted it as both a radio station song and a digital download and made a special video to show their live singing.

In November 2009 Take That released the official DVD of their Circus tour, which became the fastest-selling music DVD of all time in the UK on its first day of release. This overtook the previous record sales holder, which was Take That's Beautiful World Live tour.

Wenn

Robbie vs Gary: the frosty relationship

Throughout 1995 and 1996 Robbie Williams had been falling out with the rest of the band but in particular Gary Barlow. Williams thought that he should be the biggest star in Take That, despite the fact that Barlow was responsible for the band's lyrics and most of the overall songwriting and music. However Williams was arguably the most popular with the fans and he was drawing in the big crowds and dominating the posters and merchandising.

The two had started to fall out over Robbie Williams' excessive drinking and drug-taking which Barlow though was bad for the band's image with youngsters.

Barlow and the rest of the band confronted the record company and eventually Williams, after Robbie failed to turn up until the very last moment at the group's 1995 Brit Award performance. Robbie left the group and blamed Gary for his departure.

It was at the point the two left that they were destined not to speak again until almost 13 years later. In the meantime however things between the two became rather bitchy. Williams revealed in an interview that his first thoughts of Gary Barlow were that he "was too big for his boots and was up himself. I thought he was far too image conscious but for me his trainers looked crap". Williams later went on to criticise Barlow for being "a bland individual". He also said in a magazine interview that "Gary Barlow is a w*****. Please cut that out coz i genuinely mean it. I can't stand the man; all he does is whine and moan". Clearly Barlow became very upset and decided not to keep in touch with Williams at all. In fact the only member of the band who kept regular contact with Robbie was Mark Owen who as a result performed live on stage with Robbie at the famous Knebworth gigs.

Barlow too wasn't wholly complimentary about Williams' behaviour calling him incredibly naïve and offensive. In an interview with the Metro newspaper and Q Magazine after the pair had made up Barlow said he was still the boss of Take That. I am kind of the band's 'big brother' and 'I guess a bit of the boss as well'. 'It's funny because there's so much of that still there. I kind of still lead the trail.' Barlow also admitted he was envious of Angels singer Williams' success after he left Take That. 'F****** right I was. The thing I've learned from having Rob back in my life is that it wasn't being envious of him, it was more that I love being in the industry.' Barlow says he is desperate to cling to success now he is back in the limelight. 'I love days like today, doing a photo shoot, being driven here in a nice car. It's a nice life. And it's f****** temporary, unless you're incredibly lucky.'

In 2005, Gary appeared to offer a hand of friendship and forgiveness to Robbie at the press conference to confirm the band's future tour. Talking about the offer to go back on the road, worth a reported £1.5m to each band member, Barlow said: "Robbie has been included in the offer but I don't know what he thinks. But we would do it without him. I think we'd have to. "Our live shows were what made Take That great, so if we came back it would have to beat that otherwise I wouldn't want to do it."

In 2007 it appeared that the two had finally begun

TAKE THAT back for good

to patch things up and were starting to talk to each other again. Barlow went onto GMTV to talk about the conversation he had recently had with Williams. Robbie Williams and former Take That bandmate Gary Barlow are on speaking terms again after years of feuding. "Yes, we met. We had a great chat. He's really well and we're good buds again. It was the best meet-up we've had since 1996." However at the time Barlow denied his meeting with Williams signalled the singer planned to re-join the band. "No re-join, it wouldn't be best for either of us at the moment."

In 2008 Robbie and Gary were seen together in public for the first time since 1995 when the two attended a football match. The two sat near to each other at Arsenal's Emirates stadium in November that year for Arsenal's big game against Manchester United.

A BBC report at the time repeated the fact that they weren't intending on a reunion: The pair chatted amiably before the game, Williams even putting an arm around Barlow during a TV interview. "We've not spoken a word to each other yet," Williams joked. "We don't know how this is going to go." "It could go either way, this," added Barlow, who took his two children, Daniel and Emily, to the game. The light-hearted encounter follows the announcement this week that the reformed Take That have added extra dates to their UK stadium tour next summer. According to a tour spokeswoman, there are no plans for Williams to make any appearances with the group he left in 1995 to launch a solo career.

In 2009, both Robbie Williams and Take That were on the same bill for the first time in 13 years as they were to perform at a charity concert for Children in Need. The Daily Mail reported at the time that this would be the long awaited and speculated reunion, however it turned out that they didn't perform together but did embrace on stage.

"Robbie Williams and old bandmate Gary Barlow have stoked up the rumours Take That will reform as five. The two stars looked the picture of happiness together with Radio 1's Fearne Cotton yesterday. Robbie and Take That appear on the same bill for charity tonight. Fans are hoping the famous five will get back together but they are still keeping us guessing and have not revealed if they will reunite on stage this evening. The two met with Fearne ahead of their much-talked-about Children In Need concert at London's Royal Albert Hall.

Despite the BBC "categorically" denying rumours of a Take That reunion with all five members tonight, Robbie and Gary looked like best friends yesterday. Both acts will definitely perform separate sets on the same bill and insiders reckon they'll get together later

on for the long-awaited reunion."

The rumours started in 2010 of a potential reunion and make up between Robbie and the rest of the band when he was pictured outside a Los Angeles studio where Take That were recording their new album. The Daily Mail reported on the sighting as follows: 'Gary and Robbie have become really close and will always meet up if Gary is in LA.

'It's a great sign for Take That fans that they've been in the studio. The reunion is sure to happen, it's just a case of when they can fit it in, but this has definitely set the wheels in motion.' The two were last on stage together at the BBC Children in Need Rocks concert at the Royal Albert Hall London in November last year. Although it was rumoured that Robbie would be singing with Take That, their paths only crossed as Gary introduced his former bandmate onto the stage, but they joined a host of stars to sing at the end of the concert. Robbie left Take That in 1995 after friction between him and his band mates and manager Nigel Martin-Smith. A year later, the remaining members of the group announced that they were disbanding before they reformed in 2006 and were received with critical acclaim and worldwide success a decade later.'

In 2010, it was finally confirmed that Williams and Barlow had completely made up and planned to release a duet together. At this time it wasn't clear whether Williams would rejoin Take That but the speculation began to mount that the two were testing together to see if they could work on a tour and album for the band. They decided to release a duet single as part of Robbie Williams' compilation album "In and out of consciousness, the Greatest Hits of Robbie Williams". The duet was titled "Shame". The single was confirmed by Barlow to have been written in under an hour in an empty studio and helped both himself and Williams to draw a line under their 10 year feud after the latter left Take That. On the first day of the song being released to the radio and the media "Shame" received an unprecedented 694 plays on the radio and 153 plays on TV.

The song premiered on the Chris Moyles Radio 1 show on August 26th where both Williams and Barlow appeared to discuss the single. Barlow and Williams performed "Shame" live for the first time at the Help for Heroes concert at Twickenham on September 12, 2010. Both released a joint statement saying: 'It's great that people love Shame so much and we can't wait to perform it live for the first time at the Help For Heroes show... We hope everyone supports Help for Heroes as much as possible, it's a great bill and we are thrilled to be a part of it.' The duo performed the single on Strictly Come Dancing on October 2, 2010, and on Paul O'Grady Live on October 8. However the song failed to reach the UK number one in the singles chart peaking instead at number two on October 16th, despite its extensive promotion. It was kept off the top by the track "Forget You" by Cee Lo Green.

The video for the song caused some controversy as the two appeared to be making a jokey parody of the hit film Brokeback Mountain which depicts two gay cowboys. The video focuses on the relationship between Barlow and Williams, as well as Robbie's feelings after he left Take That in 1995 and how he felt after they reformed without him and achieved unprecedented success.

In 2010 the band announced they would be reforming for an album and world tour which would feature the original line-up including Robbie Williams. When asked about their relationship at the press conference in October, Barlow said that they had made up and were now good friends but that he believed that Robbie was always a bit of a lone wolf and might leave the band again after the tour. Asked about the future, Barlow said: "I don't know the answer to that. We agreed when we started - it's 20 years since we began, it's our 20th year for all of us - to do a one-off album and maybe a one-off tour would be a great thing this year.

But I think once we've done that, Rob will go back

TAKE THAT back for good

Wenn

to being Rob, we'll go back to being a four. I think it will resume to how it was."

So with the main problems all being solved and Robbie and Gary being back as best friends it laid the pathway towards a full reunion for Take That.

The return of Robbie and the future of the band 2010 onwards

As I have mentioned previously news and rumours had started to spread that the band were in talks about a possible reunion with Robbie Williams. After Robbie and Gary had made up, people presumed it wouldn't be long before the two started to work together again, they were right.

On 7 June 2010 the news broke of a single called "Shame" which had been written by Barlow and Williams and which would feature the vocals of both artists. This was the first time the pair had worked together since 1995 and would appear on the second greatest hits collection of Williams. The single peaked at number 2 in the UK singles chart whilst also achieving success throughout Europe.

On 15 July 2010, Robbie Williams announced he was returning to Take That. A joint statement between Williams and the group said "The rumours are true... Take That: the original line-up, have written and recorded a new album for release later this year," read the band's statement. "Following months of speculation Gary Barlow, Howard Donald, Jason Orange, Mark Owen and Robbie Williams confirmed they have been recording a new studio album as a five-piece, which they will release in November."

On news of the reunion fans were divided on whether they actually wanted Robbie back at all, with some saying that it would never last including Neil McCormick of the Telegraph: "Yesterday, the media was put on alert that a major announcement would be made by a pop band. Oh no, I thought, Jedward have split up. Well, it would have been more newsworthy than Robbie Williams re-joining Take That. The reunion of the original line up of Britain's best-loved overgrown boy band is not so much a surprise as an inevitability. It is the merger of two best-selling brands, a blockbusting money-spinner at a time when the moribund music industry needs all the blockbusters it can lay its grubby fingers on.

I don't doubt there is genuine emotion in the reunion for both the participants and audience. Williams has always been a bit of a lost soul, and indeed his very visible wounds, expressed through a complex mix of arrogance and insecurity, are at the core of his appeal. This reunion completes a prodigal son narrative, full of mutual forgiveness and redemption, with Robbie gratefully gushing about feeling "like coming home".

For fans, reunions represent a return of the old gang, an important part of their youth, comforting them with the notion that love and friendship endures, and everything will turn out alright in the end. But I can't see how this new arrangement will last. How do you squeeze all that raging talent, all that ego and anxiety, that irrepressible energy and hyperbolic verbosity into some tightly choreographed dance routines and five part harmonies? Somehow, a punning couplet in every third verse just isn't going to cut it for Williams, or his fans."

The lead single from Take That's forthcoming album Progress was announced as "The Flood" and was released 07 November, with the album released a week later on 15 November. It's already being predicted to become the group's twelfth UK number one with some bookies refusing to take bets as they believe it is so likely. The hype surrounding Williams' return has dominated the media for almost the entirety of October and it was hard to imagine the album would fail. Take That also announced that they had considered changing the name of the band to The English prior to the release of their sixth studio album. They decided against this after Williams' return to the band, choosing to maintain the name that made them famous.

On 26 October the band announced that they would be embarking on a huge UK stadium tour entitled Progress Live 2011 starting in Sunderland on 30 May, and finishing with 6 nights at London's Wembley Stadium in July 2011. They will then play at some of the biggest venues across Europe for the second leg of the tour. The UK venues include Sunderland, Birmingham, Manchester, Cardiff, Dublin, Glasgow and London.

Tickets went on sale at 9am on Friday the 29th of October, however the demand was overwhelming with all four of the ticket sites crashing as a result of excessive demand. The very same day tickets for the tour were almost sold out and some tickets were selling for three times the cost price of £55 on the auction website ebay. The band almost immediately had to announce extra dates in Birmingham, Manchester and London which would be added to the already extensive and tiring tour.

So it's come to the time to consider what the future is past the 2011 tour and album release. Will Robbie Williams stay with the band and how much longer with the other four continue to put out new material and tour? Will Take That remain the super group that they currently are?

It's hard to say what will happen although Gary Barlow has already speculated that he believes Williams will want to pursue his highly successful solo career and that the band will probably return to a four piece. Williams has been rather sketchier on the details saying "The thing is, the door is open to do whatever we want. We've got 18 months planned. Whatever happens after, whatever happens after that. We haven't decided." However whatever happens, the band will have a highly successful and lucrative tour that is rumoured to be netting each of them one and a half million pounds before endorsements and advertising. I suppose for the sake of the fans all we can say is, let's hope that Take That are around in another decade as this year marks the 20th anniversary of their career in music.

Wenn

Awards and nominations

Take That have been one of the most successful bands of all time and certainly of the last 20 years. The band have been nominated for numerous awards over the last two decades and have picked up more than their fair share of both nominations and wins. They have been prolific at the Brit Awards, the Q awards and even the highly prestigious Ivor Novello Awards for songwriting. In this section I am going to explore the awards given to Take That and the significance they had on the band's career and popularity.

Take That were first recognised for their musical talents in 1993 at the early stage of their careers in pop music. The Brit Awards shortlist was announced in February and featured a nomination for "Could it be Magic" for Best British Single. Nobody had expected the band to even be nominated and they were the rank outsiders to actually pick up the award with some bookmakers offering odds in excess of 15-1. The show was broadcast from the Alexandra Palace and hosted by former Crystal Maze presenter and Rocky Horror Picture Show creator Richard O'Brien. In the days running up to the competition the odds on the group had been rapidly falling and they went into the night as join favourites alongside Tasmin Archer's song "Sleeping Satellite". The band went on to win the award thus launching them as international superstars.

In 1994, the band returned to the Brit Award nominations after they were put forward for Best British Single again, this time for "Pray". The show was hosted by Elton John again from the Alexandra Palace in London. Take That were again victorious meaning they were the first band to win back to back Best Single in the history and the first group since Fairground Attraction to do the double since the awards were founded in 1977. They also picked up a second award for Best British Video which also went to "Pray".

1995 was a barren year for the band, which had been rocked by the Robbie Williams controversy before the band picked up again in 1996 with the infamous classic "Back for Good" receiving another Brit Award nomination once again in the category of Best British Single. For the third time in four years the band won the award, which by now had moved to the bigger venue of Earls Court and were being presented by DJ and TV presenter Chris Evans. Ultimately this was to be the band's last award pre-reformation as the band has disbanded by the next award ceremony in 1997.

During the band's ten year absence Robbie Williams did have some success in the award category picking up three awards in 1999 for Best Male Soloist, Best Video and Best British Single for "Angels" and "Millennium". He also picked up two awards in 2000 winning Best British Single and Video for "She's the One". In 2001 Williams was nominated for another 4 categories and was named Best British Soloist for the second time in three years. He also won Best Single and Video for "Rock DJ". He continued to dominate the awards for 2 more years winning Best Male Soloist in both 2002 and 2003.

Once the band reformed in 2006 there was nothing to stop them from picking up the trophies.

TAKE THAT back for good

Wenn

The group picked up their first ever Q Magazine and Music Award in 2006, when they were named the Q Idol Award winners, which is usually awarded to the band that has had the greatest impact on their genre of music, much like a lifetime achievement award. This was recognition for the band's musical achievements to date and also their future ones after the reunification.

In 2007, the ceremony was again held at Earls Court and this time hosted by comedian Russel Brand and Radio DJ and TV presenter Fearne Cotton. They were once again nominated for Best British Single but weren't the favourites to win as people thought they were too old and modern music should get its chance to shine. However their track "Patience" beat off competition from James Morrison and Amy Winehouse to grab the group their fifth Brit Award and their first in ten years.

They followed on with an amazing 4 nominations for the 2008 ceremony hosted again by Fearne Cotton but this time with the entire Osbourne family, led by Ozzy and Sharon. They were up for Best Group, Best Album, Best Single for "Shine" and Best Live Act. They managed to win the Best Single and Best Live Act award. However some critics panned the judges' decision to give the other two awards to the Arctic Monkeys instead.

However 2008 became more memorable when the band received the Ivor Novello award for their single "Shine". The award recognised lyrical talents and the importance of songwriting. The official title was the "Most performed work" award which Take That won, because their song was well crafted and thought out.

They received a further nomination in 2009 in the category of Best Group but again failed to win the award, which this time went to Elbow, who had broken through significantly and received universal praise for their album. In 2010, the Awards celebrated their 30th birthday and as such a special category was created for the Brit Album of the last 30 years. Take That got down to the final shortlist with their album of "Beatles Medley songs" but the winning album went to Oasis for "What's the Story Morning Glory".

Finally towards the end of 2010 Take That were again given an award by Q Magazine but this time in recognition of their lifetime service to music. They won the Q Hall of Fame Award which highlights those artists who have made a truly memorable and credible contribution to music over a long period of time.

In other media and merchandising

Take That have also been heavily involved in advertising, merchandising and media. You can buy almost everything from scarves, T-Shirts and hats to Take That calendars, clock, annuals and diaries. The band has become a nationwide phenomenon and has even featured in video games and films. They have been in several of the Guitar Hero and Rockband series of games developed for Playstation and Xbox and Robbie Williams has also been involved in Singstar productions.

In April 2006, Gary Barlow and EMI licensed the band's songs to be used in the musical Never Forget, a musical based on songs of the band from the 1990s. However the group later posted and then removed a statement on their website distancing themselves from it.

They have also been involved in movie production when they wrote and recorded the theme song "Rule the World" for the film Stardust directed by Matthew Vaughn, which was released in cinemas across the globe in October 2007.

Take That presented their own TV show Take That Come To Town, a variety show in which they performed some of their biggest hits. The show also featured comedy sketches with one of Peter Kay's alter egos Geraldine McQueen. It aired on 7 December 2008 on ITV1.

Showing just how global the group have become, in 2010, they appeared on the Taiwanese programme Kangxi Lai Le, where they are one of the most recognizable groups outside of Taiwan. Taiwan comes under the jurisdiction of China and for any band to be allowed to appear there is a huge coup for their music. The group were interviewed and traded jokes with the hosts.

In November 2010 ITV aired Take That: Look Back, Don't Stare, which focussed on the reunited band whilst looking back to the past and into the future.

Discography

The discography of Take That consists of five studio albums, two compilation albums, twenty-two singles, and eleven video albums.

Take That made their debut in the United Kingdom in 1991 with "Do What U Like", "Promises" and then "Once You've Tasted Love" followed in 1992. They were only minor hits in the UK. The band's breakthrough single was a cover of the 1970s Tavares hit "It Only Takes A Minute", which peaked at number seven in the UK Singles Chart. This success was followed by the track "I Found Heaven" and "A Million Love Songs", both top 20 hits. Their cover of the Barry Manilow disco hit "Could It Be Magic" gave them their biggest hit to date, peaking at number three in the UK. Their first album, Take That & Party, was also

released in 1992. The following year saw the release of second album Everything Changes. It spawned four UK number one singles; "Pray", "Relight My Fire", "Babe" and the title track "Everything Changes". The fifth single "Love Ain't Here Anymore" reached number three. Everything Changes also saw the band gain international success. In 1995 came their third album, Nobody Else, containing another UK number one, "Sure". The second single from the album, "Back for Good" would become their biggest hit single reaching number one in 31 countries around the world. In the summer of 1995 band member Robbie

Williams left the band. Undaunted by the loss, Take That continued to promote Nobody Else as a four piece, scoring another UK number one single with "Never Forget". In February 1996 Take That formally announced that they were disbanding. This was followed by the Greatest Hits compilation, which contained a new recording, a cover of The Bee Gees' "How Deep Is Your Love", the band's final number one single.

In November 2005 the band returned to the top of the UK album charts with Never Forget.

The Ultimate Collection, a new compilation of their hit singles and then in May 2006 the band announced they were reforming after ten years. The band's comeback album Beautiful World, entered the UK album chart at number one and is currently the 35th best-selling album in UK music history. The first single from the album, "Patience" was released in November 2006 and reached number one in its second week, this was followed by "Shine", another number one single. Other singles released were "I'd Wait For Life" and "Rule the World", a UK number two over the Christmas period of 2007. The first single "Greatest Day" from their next album, The Circus, debuted at number one in the UK in November 2008. The album followed a month later and also debuted at number one. Second single "Up All Night", peaked

at number fourteen in the UK which was followed by "Said It All" peaking at number nine.

In November 2009, Take That released their first live album, The Greatest Day

Take That Present: The Circus Live which reached number 3 in the UK and went platinum.

TAKE THAT AND PARTY

Released 1992

The band's debut album, it peaked at number 2 in the UK singles chart. It was released in August 1992 and managed to remain in the charts for 19 weeks. The band released a total of seven singles from the album but only three managed to make the top 20 in the UK singles charts. "Could it be Magic", which was the last single released, peaked at number 3, "A million love songs" which reached number 7 and "It only takes a minute" also peaking at number 7.

Critics were genuinely impressed by the band's debut album and hoped it was a sign of things to come. Peter Fawthrop from All Music wrote this review of the album in 2006 when the album was re-released as part of the band reunion: The album

Empics

TAKE THAT back for good

can be accurately described as more youthful than their future recordings; "A Million Love Songs" was written by lead singer Gary Barlow at the age of 15, and reached number seven on the music charts. There is a deep sensitivity in England toward Take That; the story of the group and its progress and departure was just as meaningful as the music the band produced. Hearing Robbie Williams on the tracks here, especially his lead on the cover of Barry Manilow's "Could It Be Magic," brings back a feeling of lost innocence and a perspective on the changing of times.

"I Found Heaven"

A song that wasn't actually written by Gary Barlow but by Billy Griffin and Ian Levine. It was the fifth single released from the album. It made the top 20 peaking at number 15 in the UK singles chart. It was also the first song to feature both Gary Barlow and Robbie Williams sharing the role of lead vocalist. The video for the song was filmed on Sandown Beach in the Isle of Wight and shows the band playing volleyball.

"Once You've Tasted Love"

Written by Gary Barlow, it became the third single released form the band's debut album. However it wasn't successful reaching only number 47 in the charts. The music video was also low budget and was shot in a warehouse.

"It Only Takes A Minute"

Originally a song from 1975 by Tavares and covered by Jonathon King, Take That made the song their own. It was the band's fourth single from the album and their first UK top 10 hit reaching number 7. The music video shows the band at a boxing ring trying to catch the attentions of a ring girl.

"A Million Love Songs"

The penultimate single from the album and also one of the group's most popular songs. It was written by Gary Barlow at the age of just 15. It also peaked at number 7 in the charts making it the band's second top ten hit. The group also performed the song on the 2006 final of X Factor with eventual winner Leona Lewis. It has been voted by critics as "The Greatest Ballad of all time"

"Satisfied"

An album track that was never released as a single, Satisfied was written by Gary Barlow and was 4 and a half minutes long.

"I Can Make It"

Another album track that wasn't released as a single,

also written by Gary Barlow and just over 4 minutes in length.

"Do What U Like"

Often called Take That's experiment with the genre of House music, Do What U Like was written by Gary Barlow and Ray Hedges. It was released as the album's lead single in 1991 but was a commercial failure and only reached number 82 in the chart. It is the only single not to be included in Take That's 2005 Greatest Hits album. The band didn't play the song after 1995 and it has been almost lost to the archives.

"Promises"

Written by Gary Barlow and Graham Stack it was the third single released from the album. The single did reasonably well and reached number 38 in the UK singles chart. The video is divided into 3 parts and shows them rehearsing the song, break dancing, and finally performing the song.

"Why Can't I Wake Up With You"

An album track written by Gary Barlow and was one of the longest on the album at 5 minutes. It was later released as a single on Everything Changes.

"Never Want To Let You Go"

This was an album track that wasn't released as a single, written by Gary Barlow.

"Give Good Feeling"

Another album track written by Barlow that was never released.

"Could It Be Magic"

A famous cover of a song by Barry Manilow, Could It be Magic became Take That's biggest chart success to date. The song was the final single released from the debut album and peaked at number three. The song sold over 200 thousand copies in the UK and won Best British Single at the 1993 BRITS. In the video a young woman closes up the garage she's working in, then the band arrive with a load of people. They switch the lights on and Robbie Williams begins performing the song, the other band members dance and break-dance throughout. The video ends with the woman coming back and switching the light back off, though everything is still as she left it.

"Take That and Party"

Despite being the album's title track, the group decided not to release it as a single because they had already moved onto recording new material for "Everything Changes". It was written by Gary Barlow and Ray Hedges.

EVERYTHING CHANGES

Released 1993

The album that made the band famous, it reached number one in the UK albums chart and was nominated for the 1994 Mercury Music Prize. The album was released in October 1993 to the UK market before being released in Japan and Europe. It was certified platinum no less than four times in the UK. The album contains some of the group's most well-known songs including the number one singles "Everything Changes" "Relight My Fire", "Pray" and "Babe". The other two singles released from the album were also highly successful with "Why can't I wake up with you" reaching number two and "Love ain't here anymore" peaking at number three.

Critics unanimously gave the album 4 and 5 stars reviews, with some calling it the best pop music album of its generation. Peter Fawthrop from All Music said "When the hype sets in, it is hard to distinguish the value of the material itself. It is an album of dance-pop and ballads sung by five young men, with a greater maturity than most boy band albums thanks to the writing by lead singer Gary Barlow. Boy bands have their share of sceptics, and getting those to tear down their defences usually ends up competing with their struggle to please the fan base they already have. With saucy dance tracks like "Relight My Fire" (a hit for Dan Hartman in the 70s) and quality ballads like "Pray" and "Love Ain't Here Anymore," as well as pop tracks "Everything Changes" and "Whatever You Do to Me," Take That won over everyone they needed to. What they got in return was a reputation for being a fine group with real talent. Everything Changes marked the height of Take That popularity"

"Everything Changes"

The fifth single from the album, Everything Changes became Take That's fourth consecutive number one single. The song sold in excess of 350 thousand copies and received a silver certification. The video, liberally based on Kylie Minogue's video for her single "Give Me Just A Little More Time" shows the band in a jazz cafe, Robbie sings the song and the others are dancing and engaging with the people in the cafe as they sing. The people in the cafe sing and dance also. Gary is playing on the piano and there are also jazz musicians performing their parts of the song. The lyrics were written by Barlow with Williams on lead vocals.

"Pray"

The second single from the album, Pray was Take That's first ever number one. It even managed to stay in the number one spot for 4 weeks and sold over 400 thousand copies making it also silver certificated.

The music video shows the band in an exotic location and cuts between the group jumping in and out of bollards to individual set pieces. Jason is making contact with a woman using reflective mirrors. Mark is on the beach with a woman behind him on a large pole. Robbie is with a woman who is half tree and he's holding onto the branches. Howard is by a fountain with a woman there also. Gary is shown singing the song and looking out towards the ocean. The video alternates between black and white and colour. During the final chorus with the choir the band are shown with lots of people jumping in and out from the bollards. The video was shot in Acapulco, Mexico.

The song won two awards at the 1994 BRITS for Best Single and Best Video.

"Wasting My Time"

An album track written by Barlow and not released as a single.

"Relight My Fire"

The song was sung as a duet with Lulu and reached

Wenn

UK number one in 1993 as the third single from the album. It became the second of the band's number one hits and was also Lulu's first ever number one. The song has sold over 200 thousand copies in the UK. The video starts with two people opening the doors to the club, the band then walk in, and through all the people in the club. The group is then shown throughout performing the song. When Lulu's section comes in she is first shown dancing in the club and singing. Then the band and Lulu sing the song together on the stage till the end of the song. The video finishes with the band being the last to leave the club when everyone else has gone

"Love Ain't Here Anymore"

The sixth and final single from the album, it peaked at number three in the UK singles chart. Despite this the song has still sold over 200 thousand copies in the UK. The video starts with individual portraits of the band members as they emerge out of darkness, all dressed in white. The band are shown performing the song individually. The orchestra is then lit up and shown as the violins play. The whole group is shown standing together in silhouettes before being lit up and singing up into the microphones. The band then sing together until the end of the song before disappearing, leaving the microphones.

"If This Is Love"

An album track written by Howard Donald and Dave James. It marked Donald's first foray into song-writing.

"Whatever You Do To Me"

An album track written by Gary Barlow

"Meaning Of Love"

An album track written by Gary Barlow

"Why Can't I Wake Up With You"

First heard on Take That and Party it was re-released as a single and put on the new album. It became the album's lead single and peaked at number two on the UK singles chart.

"You Are The One"

An album track by Gary Barlow

"Another Crack In My Heart"

Also an album track written by Gary Barlow

"Broken Your Heart"

Another album track written by Gary Barlow

"Babe"

The fourth single from the album and the third successive Take That release to go to number one.

It managed to knock Mr Blobby's single off the number one spot but Blobby got his revenge stealing the coveted Christmas number one from the band a week later. The single sold over 600 thousand copies.

The video starts with Mark Owen looking out over the docks. The video is cut between Mark's journey and the whole group stood singing the song around Gary playing on the piano. The video shows Mark acting out the story of the song. Mark is seen wandering through streets with his bag on his shoulder. He visits his girlfriend's house and an old man answers the door and gives Mark a number, he then calls from a phone box. Whilst this is happening his girlfriend is shown in her large house, which has snow everywhere, and she is wearing a black veil. He walks across moors and then to a pub, Howard Donald is shown cycling past him. He enters the pub and sees Robbie Williams is looking down with a drink in his hand, and Jason Orange is leaning against a wall. Mark goes and talks to Gary Barlow who points him in the right direction. He then runs towards her big mansion and enters, it's derelict and covered in snow. He finds her and they cuddle, as he looks on he sees a fancy chandelier and a little boy emerges from behind it. Mark picks him up and cuddles him, then the rest of the band emerge and play in the snow and you see the camera crew. Robbie

messes around with the clapper board and the final shot is of the band in the room with the piano, with their head in their hands or looking glum.

NOBODY ELSE

Released 1995

Take That's third studio album, it was released in May 1995 and became the band's last album before they split. The album spawned three number 1 singles: "Sure", "Back for Good" and "Never Forget". The single release of Never Forget in July 1995 marked the departure of Robbie Williams. The album reached number one in the UK. They also released a film version of the album as part of their own concert tour to promote it. This was also the first album that the band released in the United States. However the band still failed to crack the lucrative American market. Despite not receiving the same levels of critical acclaim as the previous album the album was still widely liked and given a 4 star average rating.

Bryan Buss from All Music slammed the album for its failure in the American market. "Where Hanson sparked the boy band craze in the U.S. with a

Wenn

TAKE THAT back for good

tight band, assured songwriting, good vocals, and an appreciation for rock & roll, and the Backstreet Boys and *NSYNC gave us lush harmonies and production, Take That lacks the confidence or the style of even the weakest cut by the above-mentioned groups. With lyrics like "Love ain't here anymore / it's gone away to a town called yesterday," you almost snap out of the coma the rest of the album has induced - simply because the lines are laughable. Despite lilting vocals on "Back for Good" and the surprisingly risqué "Babe," there isn't a cut that stands out on Nobody Else. Teen pop isn't always art, but it still needs to be well done and have a little bite. This album doesn't offer either."

"Sure"

This marked a departure from the band's original pop style into an R&B type song. Upon its release in 1994 it split the critics but still made UK number one. The band used the song to try and get into the American market but failed.

The video was seven minutes long and featured the band preparing for a party while Mark is putting a little girl to bed so they can party. During the video, Gary demonstrates the opening of the song to Jason while Howard is doing the organising and Robbie is out getting some food and drinks. As the friends arrive and the toy in the bedroom plays a tune, the opening plays and the song starts. The video shows all the people at the party enjoying themselves and also shots of the band performing somewhere else in string vests and doing the dance routine. Once the friends have left in the elevator the song finishes and the band and some others have crashed out on the floor of the apartment. The little girl wakes up and walks through them all, stepping over them and looking around. The song has sold over 200 thousand copies and is certified silver. The song also featured lyrics from Owen and Williams as well as Barlow.

"Back For Good"

Arguably Take That's most successful song of all time. It reached number one in Australia, Canada, Denmark, Germany, Ireland, Norway, Spain and the UK. It became the band's 6th UK number one and also their only ever career top ten in the United States.

A music video was released to promote this song. The video was shot in black and white. The group at the start are running through the rain and into a hut. Jason is playing the guitar and the others are sitting around singing the song. The sales of the single in the UK have exceeded 1 million making it one of the highest selling singles of all time. Barlow proclaimed Back For Good as one of his favourite songs and some of the best lyrics he ever wrote. The song won Best Single at the 1996 BRITS.

"Every Guy"

An album track written by Gary Barlow.

"Sunday To Sunday"

It became the first song to feature three of the band's members in collaboration. The song was written and performed with lead vocal by Barlow, Donald and Owen. However it was never released as a single despite speculation that had the band stayed together it would have been the 4th single release.

"Nobody Else"

An album track written by Gary Barlow.

"Never Forget"

It reached the top of the UK singles chart in 1995 as well as also topping charts in Ireland and Spain. It featured Howard Donald on lead vocals but was written again by Gary Barlow. It finished 4th in an NME poll of the Greatest Boy Band Records of all time. The song has sold over 400 thousand copies in the UK and achieved gold certification.

The music video starts with fans dashing through gates at a concert towards the stage and security guards patrolling to contain the crowds. The video then shows short clips of all the members of the band as children, before then showing still photographs of the members as children. The video shows a montage of the band's history including awards won, Gary accepting an award from Elton John, meeting Prince Charles and their international fans. The video also shows how their lives have changed with a barrage of fans everywhere they go and international plane journeys, as well as concert footage. The video ends with the band heading off after a concert in a van and then a clip of Gary as a child riding away on his trike. However, despite some critics calling the video a classic it failed to win the BRIT Award that year.

"Hanging Onto Your Love"

This was a collaboration between Gary Barlow and the Grammy award winning house music producer David Morales. However it wasn't released as a single.

"Holding Back The Tears"

An album track written by Gary Barlow.

"Hate It"

Another album track written by Gary Barlow.

"Lady Tonight"

A further album track written by Gary Barlow.

"The Day After Tomorrow"

The last track on the album written by Gary Barlow.

"How Deep Is Your love"
1996 single release

Take That released a single to promote their new greatest hits album shortly before the band broke up. It was a cover of the legendary Bee Gees song "How Deep Is Your Love". The song shot to number one in the midst of the speculation and confirmation the band were disbanding.

BEAUTIFUL WORLD

Released 2006

Beautiful world became the band's comeback album and their first release in a decade. The album features what Take That describe as "a throwback to the 90s, but with a modern twist". Beautiful World is their first album in which every member of the band sings lead vocals on at least one song.

The album went to number one in the charts and sold over 2 million copies. It also claimed the title of 2nd best-selling album of 2006 despite only being released in November and only being on sale for a month. 5 singles were released from the album in total and two singles "Shine" and "Patience" reached UK number one. One of the singles "Reach Out" was only released as a single in Europe and generally charted well.

Critics quite liked the group's comeback album and rated it between 3 and 5 stars. One critic said "The album doesn't try for anything too dramatic and oozes with their obvious joy and gratitude at being back at the top of their game. Hearing Gary's voice on the majority of the tracks is a comforting reminder of times past, but having the other three as lead singers provides a refreshing change, with Jason Orange's Wooden Boat standing out particularly. The songs are varied and more reflective than their previous work evoking the struggles to stick together and time passing.

Their amazing comeback single 'Patience' jostles for prominence amongst a string of epic opening tracks including 'Reach Out' and 'Hold On' (Mark on lead vocal). Then there are the beautiful ballads 'Like I've Never Loved You At All', stand out track 'I'd Wait For Life' and the pensive 'What You Believe In'.

The album gets its really interesting twist with the Beatles-esque 'Shine' and the folk-tinged 'Wooden Boat', with Jason taking his first lead vocal."

"Reach Out"

Reach Out was released for the European Union and only as an album track in the UK. However it wasn't overly successful and only made the top 20 in Denmark and Italy.

"Patience"

Patience became the first single released from the new album, almost ten years after their previous song release. The single reached the top of the charts in Denmark, Germany, Spain, Switzerland and the United Kingdom. The song was knocked off the Christmas number one spot by X-Factor winner Leona Lewis. It sold over 150 thousand copies and was certified gold. The video was directed by David Mould and was shot in Iceland. The video shows each of the members going on a solo journey holding a microphone and a stand, they trek across rough terrain during the day time. The band eventually all make it to a point by the edge of a cliff, towards the end of the song. The setting then changes to dark and the band all sing the song together, whilst water explosions occur behind them.

"I'd Wait For Life"

Released as the third single from the album, it failed to impress and only reached number 17 in the UK charts. It was their first single to miss the top ten since 1992 hit "I found Heaven". It also ended the bands streak of 6 consecutive number one singles.

"Beautiful World"

An album track written by the band in collaboration with Steve Robson.

"Hold On"

An album track written by Take That and Grammy Award winning producer John Shanks

"Like I Never Loved At All"

The song is a quite beautiful ballad that wasn't ever released as a single. It was written by Take That and John Shanks.

"Shine"

The second single from the album and arguably the most successful release since the band reformed. The song has been used for the Morrisons supermarket television adverts. It has sold almost 350 thousand copies in the UK and reached number one in February 2007. The video for "Shine" was directed by Justin Dickel with a concept of recreating a Busby Berkeley style musical number.

"Ain't No Sense In Love"

An album track written by Take That and American singer-songwriter Billy Mann.

"What You Believe In"

An album track written by Take That and Swedish Pop Idol judge and musician Anders Bagge.

"Mancunian Way"

Another album track written by Take That and E.G.White.

"Wooden Boat"

The first time that Jason Orange had taken lead vocals on a Take That song. It wasn't released as a single but has a folk like sound.

THE CIRCUS

Released 2008

The Circus was the band's fifth studio album and was released in November 2008. The band released the album at the same time as a Britney Spears album which shared the same title. The album itself reached number one in the UK album charts and was certified double platinum. Five singles were released from the album but only one track from the album reached number one "Greatest Day" which some critics said was too cheesy and actually disliked. Most critics openly favoured album tracks which the band chose not to promote as they were busy working on their Live Tour. As a result the sale of other singles after "Greatest Day", were disappointing.

Most of the reviews for the album were positive although some said they didn't like the change in Take That's traditional boy band pop music style. Stephen Thomas Erlewine at All Music gave the album 3 stars saying "The Circus builds on the band's template, offering more of the same without quite seeming like pandering. Fittingly for a foursome facing 40, dance-pop has been banished in favour of well-manicured maturity, culled chiefly from Coldplay, whose tasteful, chilly surfaces blend easily with Gary Barlow's Elton John and George Michael aspirations. Barlow is also responsible for the gentle Sgt. Pepper's pastiche of the title track, but the one responsible for giving The Circus a bit of a beat is Mark Owen, whose contributions, particularly the cheerfully respectful stomp "Up All Night," are a welcome break from the album's steady, stately march. The Circus is the work of a group where the sum is greater than the parts, and Take That have wound up with an adult pop album that is somewhat comforting but not entirely successful."

Other critics disagreed with some giving the album 5 stars and saying it was one of the great pop albums of the noughties. BBC Music said "Modern day Take That are like the drama faces of Melpomene and Thalia. Gary Barlow, the graceful swan of the group, is cementing his position as the country's premier pop writer by dripping tragedy over soaring, epic ballads. Melancholy lament What Is Love has Howard shining on lead vocals, questioning 'the science of fate' while title track The Circus says it best with "I'm the only clown you'll ever know. I love you was too many words to say". The brilliant Rule The World might be hard to top but opening track The Garden and the perky Hold Up The Light have that same magical feel. With songs like this, we're left curious why they went with the relatively lacklustre Greatest Day as lead single. However it's a stunning album, Take That are the vintage champagne of pop fizzing with playful bubbles and happily maturing with age."

"The Garden"

The third single from the album, The Garden failed to impress on the charts and only reached number 97. Some put this down to the band's lack of promotion for the single due to their focus on the tour.

"Greatest Day"

The lead single from the album, the track actually split the critics with some calling it a copy of Coldplay. The band performed the song at Children in Need in 2008 before donating 250 thousand pounds to the charity. The single has sold almost 300 thousand copies in the UK and reached number one in the charts. It became the band's 11th UK number one single. The video for "Greatest Day" was filmed on location in Los Angeles on top of a 60 storey building in the downtown area. It was directed by Meiert Avis, who previously shot videos for U2, Damien Rice, Bruce Springsteen and Bob Dylan. The band shot the video while visiting producer John Shanks in the city whilst he was mixing the album.

"Hello"

An album track written by Take That and Grammy Award winning English producer Steve Robson

"Said It All"

The fourth single from the album, "Said it all", like the Garden before it also failed to impress upon the charts peaking at number 9. However this was viewed by some as a success due again to the lack of promotion the single received. "Said It All" was written by band members Gary Barlow, Jason Orange, Howard Donald, Mark Owen and songwriter Steve Robson, who previously enjoyed a smash hit with "Shine".

"Julie"

An album track written by Take That and Steve Robson

"The Circus"

Despite being the title track for the album it was never released as a single. Some have said this is because Britney Spears' version of Circus released at the same time was highly successful and Take That didn't want to draw comparisons.

"How Did It Come To This"

An album track written by Take That in collaboration with Jamie Norton and Ben Mark.

"Up All Night"

The second single to be released from the album it peaked at number 14 in the charts. This was despite it being performed on Ant and Dec's Saturday Night Takeaway and on the last ever episode of Gavin and Stacey. However the song did become the band's 20th successive UK top 20 single.

"What Is Love"

An album track written by Take That, credited to Gary Barlow.

"You"

Another album track written by Take That

"Hold Up A Light"

A further album track written by Take That and Norton.

"Here"

The final track on the album written by the band along with Olly Knights and Gail Paridjanian

PROGRESS

Released 2010

The Progress album has been declared for release at the end of November 2010. It will also be the first album to feature Robbie Williams since 1995. A joint statement between Williams and the group said, "The rumours are true... Robbie is back... and to celebrate, we've written and recorded a new album, due for release later this year." On the same date, national newspapers printed the headline: "Following months of speculation, it has been confirmed that Robbie Williams is to make a return to Take That. Gary, Howard, Jason, Mark and Robbie have been recording a new studio album as a five-piece, which is due for release in November." Work on the album commenced in September 2009, following the final date of their sell-out Take That Presents: The Circus Live tour. Shortly afterward, it was confirmed that, 'all five members of the band had met up, to begin writing the six songs which would set the foundation for the album.' The album marks the band's 20th year in the Music Industry, as well as fifteen years since the release of the Nobody Else album, the last material the band recorded as a five-piece.

Take That have suggested that the first single to be released from the album will be a track called "The Flood" which will be released as a digital download on November the 7th. They themselves have said that the new album will be a shift away from their traditional style with less emphasis on ballad like pop and more emphasis on experimentation with electronic pop music.

On October 19th, the official track listing was announced through Take That's own website. The album will feature ten tracks in total. They are "The Flood", "SOS", "Wait", "Kidz", "Pretty Things", "Happy Now", "Underground Machine", "What Do You Want From Me", "Affirmation" and "Eight Letters". It is believed that all of the band have collaborated on the lyrics and worked closely together to develop the songs. It is also speculated that everyone will sing lead vocals at some point on the album.

The band has since announced that plans are underway for a tour in the summer of 2011. The tour is expected to include material spanning their 20 years in the music industry. The band called a press conference at 10am on October 26, 2010 in London, where they announced the Progress Live 2011 stadium tour, starting off in Sunderland at the Stadium of Light on May 30th and ending with five nights at Wembley Stadium, before playing 6 dates across Europe. In November 2010 ITV will air Take That: Look Back, Don't Stare, which will focus on the reunited band whilst looking back to the past and into the future.

In addition to the studio albums I have discussed in detail, Take That also released their first ever live album in 2009, titled "The Circus Live" the album was recorded during one of the band's Wembley gigs. The band also released five compilation albums, generally of the so called "Greatest Hits" that the band had produced in both their early and later career. These were "Greatest Hits" in 1996, "Best of Take That" in 2001, "Forever" in 2002, "Never Forget – the Ultimate Collection" in 2005 and "The platinum collection" in 2006.

Progress was the album that would finally bring the group back together. Following on from Robbie and Gary's reconciliation throughout the 2000s and their release of "Promise" they decided to get back together to release a new album as a five-piece. On 15 July 2010, it was announced that Robbie Williams would be returning to the band.

The album was finally released on the 15th November 2010 and immediately became a huge commercial success. The album received positive reviews, with most critics commending the influence

TAKE THAT back for good

of electronic music and synthesizers. It debuted at number one in the UK, becoming the second fastest-selling album of all-time. The album was originally due for release on November 22, 2010 but was brought forward a week. Barlow claimed that the decision was made after "massive pre-orders for their album" and after "analysing airplay and order data" revealing that "We've also never seen one of our singles played so much."

"The Flood" was released as the lead single in the United Kingdom on 7 November 2010. It debuted at number two in the UK, becoming the band's sixteenth top five single in the UK. In Ireland it debuted at number eight and a week later rose to number three, becoming the band's ninth top ten single in Ireland. The video features the five members of the band racing against another crew in specially-made five-seater sculling boats. The band's boat is named "Progress" after the upcoming album, whilst the band wear old-fashioned white rowing kits, bearing a custom-designed Take That crest. The group are shown to be competing in a race against a younger crew and although losing the race, the group continue going past the finish line and are shown to row down the River Thames past famous London landmarks before fading away into a stormy sea.

Critics have been universal in their praise of both the single and the album saying that it represented a significant change from Take That's traditional style of music and lyrics. A critic from the BBC said "If the title of Progress suggests the band's new sound will be a merging and evolving of Take That Mk.II and recent Robbie Williams fare, the reality is startlingly different. Progress is something entirely new – Take That Mk.III – and the strangest, most ambitious and most exciting record its creators have ever been involved in."

"The Flood"

As detailed before this was the album's first single to be released and got a huge amount of commercial and BBC radio airplay. The band did massive promotional tours and events which paid off taking them to number one in the UK singles charts.

"SOS"

Described as being like an experiment with electro rock, the song marks a huge change from Take That's traditional ballad like style of music. It's written by Mark Owen and Robbie Williams and features extensive use of synthesisers.

"Wait"

Some have expressed their delight to finally get an album track that is a classic Take That piano and strings number but even this track is deceptive. The "nice" instruments have been replaced by more "nasty" beats and electro guff. It also features Robbie Williams on lead vocals for the first time since the 1995 departure.

"Kidz"

Sounding a little bit like a combination of Take That meeting the Kinks with an almost Sunny Afternoon-esque beat to the song. I still think this could become a decent single release though as it typifies a Take That song that will grow on you with time.

"Pretty Things"

Perhaps the most distinguishing feature of the song is Robbie Williams' reasonable attempt at performing the song in a falsetto voice. A slightly cringe crooner of a song.

"Happy Now"

A very odd deeper voiced lyrical bass line and again heavily featuring synthesisers, keyboards and the electro style. However it doesn't seem to typify the traditional Take That audience.

"Underground Machine"

An upbeat song about relationships when boys meet girls and how they deal with it. However it too contains strong undertones of electro music and synthesisers as well.

"Eight Letters"

Eight Letters was written by Gary Barlow but is perhaps most famous for sampling the 1980s Ultravox hit "Vienna" and was co-written by Midge Ure, Chris Cross, Warren Cann and Billy Currie.

Wenn

TAKE THAT back for good